AN AUTHOR'S GUIDE TO GOODREADS

HOW TO NETWORK WITH MILLIONS OF READERS

BARB DROZDOWICH

Bakerview Consulting

Fifth Edition

Previously published as "The Ultimate Goodreads Guide for Authors", Barb Drozdowich, 2014

ebook ISBN: 978-1-988821-84-9

paperback ISBN: 978-1-988821-83-2

Created with Vellum

They say "It takes a village to raise a child" - it certainly takes a village to publish a book. This book is dedicated to my "village."

CONTENTS

NOTE OF THANKS

I would like to thank you for buying one of my books!

I tend to focus on the technical tasks that authors and bloggers need to learn. As of this publishing I have 27 books in print and several more in various stages of completion. I'm always looking to be helpful - often creating books around subjects that I get a lot of questions on from authors just like you.

At the end of this book is the link join my group of readers and get some free help with various technical subjects.

On to the book - I hope you enjoy and learn a lot!

PREFACE

I feel that Goodreads is best learned by experiencing – by practicing. As I say in various parts of this book, Goodreads is somewhat of a rabbit's warren filled with little gems of functionality. As authors, especially when we are first starting, we need to network. We need to find our audience. As my kids would say – find your peeps.

There are many different ways to find an audience. One can advertise, but why not take advantage of free platforms – especially a free platform with 90 million readers. Add to that fact that Goodreads' readers come from every country of the world and read all sorts of genres and you have a platform that is certainly worth exploring.

As an author, you need to set goals that are appropriate for your career. My goals are to focus on networking with my audience in every country of the world, not just my local neighborhood. Because of my goals, Goodreads is a great place for me to find friends because of its multinational nature.

To move back to my first comment about learning Goodreads by experiencing it – I have created a course – a collection of screencasts that will visually walk you through each topic discussed in this book.

You'll learn how to open an account, create an author profile, set up a giveaway, etc. **The course is free** and meant to be taken at your leisure. Once you log in, you can come back to the screencasts as many times as you choose. Do one screencast a day, or power through all of them immediately – whatever suits your learning style. To get the course, click here or copy this link (http://the-author-s-technical-help-desk.teachable.com/p/author-guide-to-goodreads) into your browser or visit my website (http://bakerviewconsulting.com) and navigate to the page for "*An Author's Guide to Goodreads: How to Network with Millions of Readers*" (http://bakerviewconsulting.com/authors-guide-goodreads-network-millions-readers/). You will find the link there. If you have difficulty accessing this free course, please send me an email at barb@bakerviewconsulting.com.

The main goal of this book and course is to share my love of Goodreads with you. I hope that you come to understand why I like Goodreads so much and I hope that you find networking opportunities that work with your personality and your book's genre.

I wish you success. Drop me a note to let me know what you think. My complete contact information is at the back of this book.

INTRODUCTION

Welcome to ***An Author's Guide to Goodreads: How to Network with Millions of Readers***.

Goodreads is ***the*** candy store for readers. It has been described as the place where insatiable readers, book bloggers, and book buyers hang out. The website has more than 90 million registered users (the last time they announced their account holder totals) and almost all of its features are completely free. What better place to interact with the potential readers of your books than this reader heaven?

My name is Barb Drozdowich. I'm a book blogger, voracious reader, technical trainer, and the author of 27 books designed to help authors and book bloggers with the various technical aspects of book promotion.

Let's talk about the elephant in the room. I've heard complaints about Goodreads. Complaints ranging from difficulties navigating the site, to bad behavior from authors and reviewers. I'm not here to criticize; I'm here to educate. I've seen examples of some of the bad behavior that has occurred.

Not nice!

I'm certainly not justifying any bad behavior that occurs, but one has to understand that Goodreads is like any other place where large groups of people hang out. Not everyone subscribes to the "If you don't have anything nice to say, don't say anything at all" philosophy.

Yet, it's important to recognize that for a reader, Goodreads is a glorious place where pretty much everyone is a book lover. With just a mouse click, readers on the Goodreads site can find up-and-coming authors with books that they may never have otherwise discovered. The geeky side of me LOVES the mobile app that allows me to walk into my local bookstore with my smartphone rather than my binder bursting full of lists of books read (yes, I used to do that) to find my next outstanding read!

For authors, Goodreads can be a free place to passively advertise your books. I've already mentioned that Goodreads boasts 90 million book lovers all in one place. It also has 12,340 book clubs from every country in the world and thousands of groups that specialize in every genre and subject under the sun. What better place to gush about the latest new book than surrounded by 90 million like-minded readers.

However, authors must keep in mind that Goodreads is NOT the place for the hard sell. One has to consider the culture of the site. You wouldn't walk into a public library and start shouting about your book. The same applies to Goodreads. Just like there is expected behavior in a library, there are expectations for how you will use the site.

I can't count the number of people who try to hit me up to review their book, which is clearly (from my bio) not something I would ever consider. People who have only one book on their shelves (their book) are not someone I'm interested in friending. We'll talk about the various activities available on Goodreads and how you can participate as a booklover. But like all social media platforms, people who only say "Buy my book" are quickly tuned out.

One of the challenges of Goodreads is that it *really* is awkward to learn to navigate. In a previous edition of this book, I tried to include screenshots to help with understanding, but the screenshots were just not helpful when viewed on smaller screens. To help you with the navigation this time around, I've created a course (http://the-author-s-technical-help-desk.teachable.com/p/author-guide-to-goodreads) that will visually walk you through the site and various actions that we will talk about. Keep your eyes open for mention of specific videos throughout the various sections.

I believe that Goodreads has a lot of underutilized gems of opportunity. I hope to help you better understand how to, not only navigate the website but have it be a valuable and powerful part of your author platform.

Learning about Goodreads is a visual and experiential activity. I am hoping that you will, at times, have your Kindle in one hand while sitting in front of your computer, walking through the steps in this book. Just reading about it or watching a video is not enough, in my opinion. You need to experience it and you need to practice it.

In the next few chapters, we are going to talk about the generalities of the personal profile and author profile, followed by an overview of the site and navigation of its various features. Once that is done, I'll lead you through the process of setting up a personal profile and then we'll create an author profile.

Like many other sites that exist on the Internet, Goodreads is always changing. There are periodic additions or subtractions to the site. Perhaps Goodreads has done this to try to make the site more friendly in terms of navigation. They are always tweaking. Goodreads offers a variety of ways to keep abreast of the changes that are occurring. I would encourage you to subscribe to their various newsletters and also subscribe to their blog to keep up to date. I try to keep this book up to date as well. This book has been changed so many times to reflect platform changes I have lost count.

I do recognize that using sites that are always in a state of change is a challenge. However, once you are confident with the various functionalities that Goodreads offers, changes in the layout should only give you momentary pause until you find your virtual footing.

1

NETWORKING

There is a lot of advice surrounding Goodreads and how to use it as a selling tool. I don't agree with all of it since I find that a softer approach tends to be more effective. Both in terms of selling books and my business, I find that the hard sell routine can turn people off. Conversely, I feel if you treat people fairly and ethically, they will respond in kind.

It makes me happy to refer books I LOVE to my readers on my book blog. Similarly, I work hard at creating helpful tutorials for my business blog. When I get a comment about how I saved someone's time, it makes my day.

I try to combine these two tactics when on Goodreads. On one hand, I'm a voracious reader and enjoy sending someone in the direction of a great book. I hope they will return the favor as I'm always looking for something new to read! I also enjoy sharing information with people that I "meet" on Goodreads. I'm happy to answer a question if I can or point someone in the right direction for what they are searching for.

This is all part of networking, which I emphasize a lot in my consulting. Building friendships and fostering relationships is key to building a business. My audience isn't as big as some authors so I take advantage of any networking opportunities I can.

Many authors gravitate towards the hard sell – the big numbers. They are only interested in the BookBub promotions and the like. They have a game plan that tends to be 'go big or go home.' There are many different ways to sell books and as an author, you need to do what feels right for your career. But when you are just starting, you don't qualify for the big promotions and it takes time to find other authors to collaborate with. Because of this, I try to get new authors to focus on being as complete with the development of their platform as possible – don't just put in the minimum required information – be thorough and as complete as possible. More on this later as I discuss what makes for a standout author profile.

As I've said before, I tend to look at the world of book promotions from a different perspective than many. I view it strategically by focusing on stats where others focus on feelings. I view book promotion as a big puzzle and I work to put as many pieces in place as I can.

I see Goodreads as a land of opportunity for authors. It comes with 90 million readers and authors. Although there are some exceptions, basically everyone on Goodreads reads. No other social media has the same concentration of readers. In the early days, I set out to see how I could connect with other readers. I had been successful in networking my book blog and I wanted to see what networking opportunities I could find on Goodreads as an author.

I found the motherlode!

In addition to walking you through the creation of an account and your author profile, this book will explain best practices for building friendships and relationships on Goodreads as I want you to look at each section with an eye towards networking.

Not every section will resonate with every author. There are parts of Goodreads that just don't work for me, but keep an open mind. Try new things. Be the creative person that I know you are. And don't hesitate to drop me an email and share your ideas!

2

DIFFERENCES BETWEEN A PERSONAL AND AUTHOR PROFILE

Goodreads offers readers the opportunity to create personal profiles and authors the chance to create an author profile. Although they are separate activities, once the two profiles are created, they are melded together. An author has all the "reader" functionality that is given to everyone who sets up a personal profile, but they also have "special powers."

To quote from the site:

> "Any author, anywhere in the world, can join the Goodreads Author Program for free. All you need is an Internet connection and a published book (or a soon-to-be-published book) that can be found in our database. The Goodreads Author Program allows published authors to claim their profile page to promote their book and engage with readers. Once verified, your author profile will include the official Goodreads Author badge, which you can use to tell your fans to follow you on Goodreads."

This is quite a different philosophy from LibraryThing or Booklikes (the other players in the reader/author/book world), all of which either frankly or subtly let authors know that their promotion is not welcome.

That being said, as I've mentioned before, the authors that have the most positive experience on Goodreads go in as a reader and don't try the hard sell routine on readers.

Let's talk about Goodreads in generalities. Goodreads allows members to create a personal account, list books, assign them to virtual shelves, join groups, and participate in events and giveaways. They use the book information that members add to make recommendations of what to read next. They allow authors to list their books, host giveaways, make friends, attract followers, and even hook up their blog feed so their fans can keep up to date.

These are important things in a reader's world as well as an author's world. In today's publishing environment, authors need to figure out ways to connect with readers the world over.

Well-respected authors have written articles over the years about why authors should have a presence on Goodreads. When I was researching for the first edition of this book, I found one such article from late 2013 and the author was claiming that Goodreads had 20 million members and 210 million books added to shelves. The most current numbers are 90 million members and 2.6 billion books. That's quite an increase in such a short time.

It is accepted by the industry and backed up by numerous articles that Goodreads is seen as a more impartial place for book lovers than the various retail sites. There are mounting concerns about the veracity of reviews on sites like Amazon or Barnes & Noble, but Goodreads reviews are seen as more honest. Sometimes the thoughts that readers share are harsh, but it is viewed as the place to find the most unbiased reviews.

Unlike other social media platforms, which are part of your author platform, everyone on Goodreads is a reader—something that isn't necessarily true on Facebook, Pinterest, or Twitter.

Many authors I talk to accept that Goodreads should be part of their platform, but are frustrated by their problems navigating the site. I believe that one thing that makes navigating Goodreads confusing for many people is that the same point on the site can be accessed using multiple methods. This is not a linear site but is in fact more complex than that.

Although there is a lot to learn about the Goodreads site, just moving through it is a learning exercise. Because of the many concerns I have heard about the navigation of Goodreads, I'm going to walk you step by step through the major activities of this site. Before we tackle the project of creating a personal account and an author profile, we are going to do an overview of the site and navigation. After that, we'll talk about other features that Goodreads offers, and most importantly, the reasons to pay attention to all the bells and whistles they offer.

As I walk you through all the variations of navigation, always keep in mind that clicking on the **Home link** on the menu bar (upper left) or the **Goodreads icon** to the left of it will always bring you back to the beginning so you can start again.

Parts of this book are meant to be a discussion of the "whys" you do certain things on Goodreads, but other sections are meant to help you walk or navigate through various actions on Goodreads. As I've said previously, I hope that you will, at times, have your Kindle in one hand while you sit in front of your computer and walk through the steps in this book.

My last point before moving on to the nuts and bolts of our subject matter is to state the intent of this book. Ultimately, it is to appeal to all authors, from beginners to the more experienced. You may find some information here that is a review for you. Are there a lot of blog posts you can cobble together to find out much of this information? Likely. If you are the type of person that likes all your reference information in one place, and if you don't revel in the Google hunt for correct information, then you are in the right place. On to the next chapter.

3

GOODREADS NAVIGATION AND CONTENT OVERVIEW

Before we start describing all the bells and whistles that Goodreads offers, I want to take some time and do an overview of the site. If you already have an account on Goodreads—either as an author or as a reader—log in and take a walk with me. If you don't have an account yet, watch the first screencast of the course mentioned at the beginning of this book and get oriented. You can also come back to this chapter after creating a new Goodreads account.

The Landing page, or what I will call the Home page on Goodreads, is what you "land" on once you log into Goodreads—either as an author or reader. The information on the Home page is meant to keep you up to date on what your "friends" are up to and also provide you with links to get to other parts of the site.

Study what you see right away after signing in. The content on the main portion of the Home page is often called the Newsfeed. The Home page intends to be helpful without being overwhelming. This page is also responsive to the width of your screen. The narrower your screen, the less information you are presented with. For example, unless I extend my browser window to the full width of my laptop screen, I don't see the three columns described below; I only see two. Keep this in mind when looking at your computer screen.

Let's visually divide the Home page into three columns. The information in the center is the Newsfeed and can be modified by the gear icon (with the label of "customize") at the upper right of the area. If this is something you pay attention to, modify it to suit your needs. On either side of the Newsfeed there is a collection of information from your content as a reader. Depending on what information you have entered, you may see the books you have marked "Am Reading;" you may see an advertisement or two; you may see a recommendation or two, and you will likely see a small menu at the bottom of one of the sides.

We are going to move from the main body of the page to the top. There is a menu bar that runs along the top of the page with "Home," "My Books," "Browse," and "Community" moving from left to right. After those words, there is a search field that will allow you to search the site for books (you can also search by author name). This search field will allow searching of the entire Goodreads site—not just your books. On the far right of this menu-line are five items. The furthest to the right is a circle that shows your photo (or a Gravatar if you haven't entered a photo yet). This photo can be clicked to show a hidden menu. We'll talk about that later. Moving to the left, you will see a circle with a person, an envelope, a chat icon, and a bell. If there is a number in a red square for any of these icons, there is something you need to pay attention to. The person in the circle icon represents friend requests, the envelope indicates direct messages you have been sent, the chat icon indicates ongoing conversations and the bell indicates notifications you have haven't looked at yet.

For those of you who get frustrated (or lost) navigating the Goodreads site, remember that the Goodreads icon and the "home" button are on every page and will always bring you back to the home screen.

You will find out as we go through the rest of this book, Goodreads has a lot of little nooks and crannies—a lot of functionality to offer to readers and authors. With the latest reorganization, the functionality has been grouped. What used to be extensive lists of menu items has been grouped by type. All of the items under the "Browse" menu item have to do with browsing for books or information. All of the items under the "Community" menu item have to do with available group activities. Lastly, all of the items under your photo on the far right have to do with *your* settings and activities. For example not just groups, but *your* groups—not just recommendations, but *your* recommendations.

The last remaining button to mention is the "My Books" button. Many authors find this misleading as it has nothing to do with the books they have published. This connects with access to the books they have indicated reading, the books they have put on shelves, the books they have reviewed or rated.

In the next chapter, we will walk through the process of opening a new account. Even if you already have a Goodreads reader/personal account, have a quick read or watch the screencast, as you will likely learn something new!

4

PERSONAL ACCOUNT

The starting point of creating a presence on Goodreads is to open an account. Readers can set up a "Personal" Profile. Authors can set up both a "Personal" Profile and an "Author" Profile. Anyone joining Goodreads must start with a Personal Profile and then they can add Author Information second—no different from the situation on Facebook with a personal profile and a business/author page.

Although setting up a Goodreads personal account is fairly straightforward, it is really important to be as complete as possible in the information you provide. As I mentioned at the end of the previous chapter, if you already have a personal account, you can either skip this section or read through to see if you have missed anything important. You can also watch the screencast for this that are part of the course attached to this book.

To open your "Personal" account, start at http://goodreads.com and click on "Sign up." There are two basic routes to signing up. You can either provide your email address and a password, or you can choose to sign in with your Facebook, Twitter, or Google identity. I generally suggest that people sign up using one of their social media platforms, as once the account is confirmed, the next step is to find friends from various sources. Facebook, Twitter, and Gmail are three possible choices. If you have chosen to log in using your Facebook credentials, your Facebook account will already be attached.

I've heard concerns from authors about using one social media profile to sign up for another. This is a valid concern for some. If you share this concern, sign up using an email address and password, as social media accounts can always be connected after the fact.

Regardless of which you choose, once you click on "Sign up," an email will be sent to the email address you provided (or your email account attached to the social media platform you chose), asking you to confirm your account. You can continue without confirming your email, although you will have to confirm it at some point.

The first page you are brought to is a page where you are allowed to find your friends. Your progression through the initial set up pages will be indicated on the progress bar along the top of this page. You will notice that the four steps you will work your way through are:

1. Find Friends
2. Set a Goal
3. Rate Books
4. View Recommendations

On this first page, you will be encouraged to find friends from various sources that are already on Goodreads. The sources of friends range from Facebook to Twitter to Gmail or Yahoo Mail.

Although you can click on the "Skip this Step" link, remember that you are joining Goodreads to be social—to network. I encourage you to take advantage of the ability to find friends from your other social media accounts. Think of it this way, if the first thing you do on Goodreads is to locate some friends, it will seem like a friendly place. Somewhat like at a cocktail party, you find a familiar face, and your comfort level increases.

When you are finished, move to the next page. "Set a Goal"

refers to the Goodreads Reading Challenge. Goodreads has a reading challenge functionality that allows you to set a numerical goal of books to read in a calendar year, and then will help keep track of your progression. We'll discuss the advantages of a Reading Challenge later in the book, but for now, choose the number of books you would like to read this year and take the challenge! As before, you can click on the "Skip this Step" link, but I encourage you to be a participant in the Goodreads community.

The third step you are lead through is "Rate Books." This is where you will share your reading tastes. In the first part of the section, you will choose your favorite genres. Remember, you are filling out *your* "Personal" profile as you, the reader. So, as a reader, choose your favorite genres to read. The reason you are doing this is to help Goodreads make better book recommendations to you and customize your browsing experience. In my opinion, being a member of Goodreads as a reader is a great experience. All the book recommendations I get are spot on, always a great suggestion of what to read next!

Once you have finished choosing genres, click "Continue" and you will be presented with a screen that will allow you to rate some books. The selection you are presented with are representative books in the genres you have chosen on the previous page, typically the most popular books of the genres you indicated. In this step, rate at least twenty titles (by clicking on the appropriate number of stars) and/or indicate some that you are interested in reading (by clicking on the green 'Want to Read' button). In common with other social media, Goodreads is a place to interact and socialize. I am suspicious of people who want to friend me and have not indicated any books. I will come back to this point when we talk about shelves, but for now, rating books and indicating the ones you wish to read is part of the social aspect of Goodreads.

The fourth step is called "View Recommendations." If you have given the Goodreads algorithms enough information, you will see some recommendations. If not, you will in the future if you continue to participate.

This is the last step in the initial section of the account setup. From here we will move to record the personal information for your account. Although you can get to that point by clicking on the "Done here, See what's next" link in the bottom right, you can also go to the upper right and hover over the person icon on the far right and click on "Account Settings."

5

ACCOUNT SETTINGS

To find your "Personal" profile information, start from the Home screen and look to the upper right corner. Click on the icon of a person in the far right and choose "Account Settings" from the choices in the drop-down menu (near the bottom of the list).

> ***Advanced note:*** *If you have already completed this step, to see the information we are going to walk through, you actually have an extra step. You will have to click on the "edit my user profile" link after you have clicked on "Account Settings" as instructed above.*

This will bring up a screen that has a series of menu tabs along the top with the first one being "Profile" and the last one being "Seller Account." We will be working our way through each menu tab, one by one, starting with "Profile." Feel free to follow along with the written information in this chapter in the screencast that is part of the course that accompanies this book.

Profile Information

When you are setting up your profile information, be as complete as you are comfortable being. You are using Goodreads as a reader and as an author. You want to network with people of like interests to give readers a point of connection. Whether it is your love of kitties and puppies or your interest in travel to the south of France, make a point to share.

Starting in the upper right, click the "Add photo to your profile" box. This will bring up a screen that will allow you to add a profile picture. Use your official author photo, or if you are writing under a pen name and trying to hide your real identity, the Gravatar that you use to represent you. You can add more than one photo if you wish, but, at a minimum, add one profile picture. If you have already started this process and are reviewing the content, you likely already have a profile photo. Note that you can delete/change that photo as well as add more photos. Once that is done, move down the list of fields, filling in the information requested. For a Username, I'd suggest using your first and last name. This will create a custom URL for your Goodreads Profile. My full name is Barb Drozdowich, which makes my custom URL:

http://goodreads.com/barbdrozdowich.

This is easy to remember and easy to connect with my books. If you have a more common name, you may have to be creative, but try to keep your username as simple and obvious as possible.

Fill in your birthdate if you want Goodreads to wish you a Happy Birthday. If you don't want this information to be common knowledge, select the appropriate choice from the drop-down below the birthdate field. Fill in your website/blog address, complete with http://, and a few words about your interests. Make sure you indicate what type of books you like to read, what genres you like best, and include a short biography at the bottom (this can be your official author biography). If you click on the "Tips" prompt, there is some help available.

Once this page is complete, go to the bottom and click on "Save Profile Settings."

6

SETTINGS TAB

Moving along the line of tabs at the top of the page to the right, we will look at the "Settings" tab next. Again, you can follow along with this information in the similarly labeled screencast that is part of the course accompanying this book.

The first thing you see on this page is your email address (and it should say "verified") & you should be able to see an encoded version of your password. This is where you can change where your email notifications are delivered to. Likewise, if you want to change your password, this is where that change can be made.

The first section of this page covers privacy issues. I would suggest that you don't have your profile completely locked down. As I have said before, you are on Goodreads to network and find friends. That isn't going to happen if no one can read anything about you. You'll also notice that Goodreads reminds you that search engines index their site. You can decide if you want Goodreads sharing with their partner sites any reviews you might create. The list of retailers they share with is changeable, but it is a way to get your name out to various retailers with your thoughts on some books. It is also a way to help your fellow authors—reviewing their books so that your thoughts can appear to help sway buying decisions in some of the minor retailers.

I would suggest you limit who can send you a private message and who can see your actual email address simply because the world has creepy people in it, sadly.

Under the section labeled "Friend" requests, I don't suggest that you add a challenge question for friends. We will talk more about friends in a future chapter, but I'll remind you again the reason you are on Goodreads is to make friends and network. Limiting your friends to your actual real-life friends is counter-productive.

The last section on this page is labeled "Site Customization." There is a checkbox asking if you want to be prompted to recommend books to friends. I would encourage you to check this box. The reminder is good and you can always say "no." Once you have made the choices you want, click on the "Save Account Settings" button at the bottom of the page to save your choices.

7

EMAILS TAB

This tab brings up a page containing a collection of settings that many people ignore. Goodreads sends out **a lot** of notifications potentially, and if you don't want your inbox filled, please look through this information carefully and choose what you want to receive. I will add my two cents in a couple of areas. You may find that you come back to this area after using Goodreads for a while to refine your choices.

This page is divided into five sections: "Mail from Friends," "Event Notifications," "Comment and Action Notifications," "Newsletters & Other Mail," and finally "Group Email Preferences." As I'm sure you are realizing, you have the potential to get a lot of notifications if you don't specify what you are truly interested in. Make your choices carefully. If you are not planning to check Goodreads regularly, you will need to keep track of what is happening there. But having your inbox flooded with emails won't help you look at Goodreads fondly!

"Mail from Friends" concerns reviews your friends have posted. As a book blogger, I'm always interested in what others are reading and what they think of that book. But honestly, I don't want this information in my inbox every day, so I choose a digest once a week that I can scan through.

The "Event Notification" section allows you to pick and choose what you want to be told about. Some of these things, like recommendations and events—we will discuss in chapters 18 & 19, so you may wish to re-visit this section after you understand what everything is.

The "Comment and Action Notification" section will allow you to choose what you want to learn about concerning these two functions. Like the previous section, you may wish to revisit this area after we have discussed some of the topics mentioned on this list so that you can make an informed choice.

The "Newsletters and Other Email" section allows you to choose what you want to receive in notifications about the various types of newsletters Goodreads offers. We will discuss these newsletters and other forms of advertising Goodreads offers in chapter 20. Again, you may wish to revisit this area once you have learned more about these functions.

The last section is notifications from the activity of "Groups" that you may be part of. If you are just starting, you aren't part of any Groups. We will discuss Groups in chapter 19 and as an advance note of warning, it's great to join active groups, but in many cases, it's not necessary to receive an email for each and every action of the group—often a daily or weekly digest is sufficient.

Although I started this chapter with the comment about this tab being the one that many people ignore, studies have shown that a large number of people claim to be overwhelmed by the number of email they receive. I know I'm in that group. Generally speaking, many of the subscription type emails we receive can be "unsubscribed" from. That is true of Goodreads notes also. In other words, people don't need to find this Emails Tab to stop the flood of notes from Goodreads. Knowing what I do about human nature (and email overwhelm) I suspect a large portion of Goodreads account holders have found a way to stop the flood.

8

FEEDS TAB

The "Feeds" Tab or page will allow you to include or exclude various pieces of information on your Update Feed or "Newsfeed." Just to remind you, the Update Feed or Newsfeed can be viewed on your home screen. It is the information that occupies the center of that page. It isn't something that is emailed to you, but the information exists, and you are welcome to read or scan it when you log in.

Because this information doesn't end up in my inbox, I find I don't worry as much about limiting what will appear. Like the other sections, go through and uncheck as you wish. Some of the items we will discuss in a future chapter, and you may wish to revisit this section. But remember—you are on Goodreads to network, so sharing your activity with your friends is a good thing!

9

APPS TAB

As its name suggests, this tab deals with Goodreads Apps. You'll see that the page is set up in a series of small areas in two columns. The ones that run down the left side of the page allow you to connect your Goodreads account with other social media accounts. The ones that run down the right side of the page are what I consider apps.

As I mentioned earlier, I encourage you to connect your Goodreads account to your Twitter account. I suggest this for two reasons. The first reason is so you can share your activity from Goodreads with your friends on Twitter easily. If you leave a review for a book, you can send a Tweet about it. The second reason is to help you find friends on Goodreads. It is possible to find friends from Twitter that also have a Goodreads account. The thought is, if they are your friend/follower on another social media, they would be happy to do the same on Goodreads.

All that being said, I hope you decide to join your Twitter account if you haven't already done so. Go through the checkboxes and select or deselect as needed.

Below this section is the area that gives you the ability to connect your Goodreads account to your Google account and your Amazon account. I don't see the usefulness of connecting to Google, and I choose to keep my Amazon identity separate from my Goodreads identity. I know Amazon owns Goodreads, but I choose to not offer Amazon the connection ability between the two.

Looking down the right side of the Apps area, you are given the ability to install a Goodreads App on your iPhone or Android phone. I suggest doing this for a number of reasons. I'm a voracious reader. I have a lot of difficulty keeping track of the books I read and the books I want to acquire from a store, or the library. As you will learn, it is very easy to create a list of books you are looking for and create a shelf for them. The next time you're at a used bookstore or the library, you can bring up the list of books on your phone as you wander through the shelves. If you can imagine, I used to keep a binder of lists of books. I'm quite certain the owner of our local used bookstore thought I was an idiot when I would wander in with my overflowing binder....

The last item concerns the ability to attach your Blogger blog to your Goodreads account. It is possible to post your book reviews from Goodreads to your blog. I choose not to do this, but if you create a lot of reviews on Goodreads and blog on Blogger, it's a time saver to post them to your blog at the same time. If this functionality interests you, play with it and see if you can adapt it to suit your needs.

10

WIDGETS TAB

The next tab we will look at is the Widgets tab. I must admit upfront one of my most favorite things about Goodreads is the variety of widgets they offer. In my experience, however, the widget code does not always display nicely on all blog themes.

The widgets we will discuss in this chapter are the reader widgets. Goodreads also offers author widgets as part of the author dashboard, and we will discuss them separately.

I just love putting a widget on one of my sites to show off the books I've read or the new releases I'm eagerly anticipating.

Goodreads widgets are fairly straightforward to use. I have a video that walks through the process as part of the course that is associated with this book as well as part of my Bakerview Consulting YouTube channel. The link to the channel is at the end of this book. Using the widgets is fairly straight forward. Pick one of the widget types available, make some choices—number of books, the width of the widget, etcetera—and then in a couple of cases, click on a button to have the code created. Copy the code and paste it in a text widget/gadget on the sidebar of your blog. (for the email widget, the code is used in your email program) Sadly, this code does not work on a WordPress.com blogs but it does work on WordPress.org, Blogger, and a couple of other platforms. WordPress.com has a work-around, however.

Take a few moments and look through the selection offered. There is something for everyone from an email signature widget to a status update widget. My favorite is called a "Custom Widget." This widget allows the display of a selection of books. You choose to include or exclude information, offer up a title, and then click on "Save Changes." Under the "Save Changes" button is a window of code. Copy all that code and paste it in a text widget/gadget on your website and magically you can share with visitors of your blog. As I mentioned above, if putting code on your sidebar is an intimidating activity for you, I have created a video to walk you through the steps as part of the free collection I offer on my Bakerview Consulting YouTube channel as well as part of the screencasts that are in the course associated with this book.

When you get a chance, play with some of the offerings in the widget selections. You may find that author widgets are more to your liking, but regardless, share your books with your readers!

As I mentioned at the beginning of this section, the widgets display on blogs by using code. Code, by definition, is something that has to be read and expressed by a blog, not like a picture that is either there or not there. Sometimes there are aspects of the coding of your blog's theme that will interfere with how the widget displays on your sidebar. If this happens, don't be afraid to ask for some help.

11

BOOK LINKS, PURCHASES AND SELLER ACCOUNT

The last three tabs are "Book Links," "Purchases" & "Seller Account." Most people don't realize that you can customize the buy links you see when you are looking at a book on Goodreads. You can purchase a book right from within your Goodreads account.

For the sake of convenience, it is possible to personalize which 'buy' links appear with the books you look at. I like to customize mine so I am not presented with a whole bunch of "buy" links I will never use. This section allows you to do that. For example, I only purchase from Amazon (I have a kindle) and I like to check availability at my local library. When I look at the listing for a book I'm interested in, the only buy links I'm presented with are Amazon.ca and a couple of libraries. I find my customized choice to be less overwhelming than being presented with a long list.

The "Purchases" tab will list any purchases made through Goodreads. In the past, I would periodically purchase advertising through Goodreads. I can keep track of what I've spent and when. I could use this section to access the area where I input the credit card I used to pay for the charge on this page. We will discuss advertising in a future chapter, but the self-service advertising that I purchased in the past is no longer available to authors.

The last tab is labeled "Seller Account." When I wrote the first version of this book several years ago, Goodreads said the tab would be removed shortly as there was no intention of allowing authors to sell ebooks. Here we are several (7) years later and several updates of this book later and I finally see that this tab is blank. I am assuming that at some point in the future Goodreads will remove this tab entirely.

Check Your Progress

Lastly, you need to check your "Personal" Profile to make sure everything is correct. You can do this by clicking on the "View my Profile" link in the upper right-hand corner. This will enable you to see it the same way everyone else will. Viewing your profile like this allows you to proofread your work. One thing I want to point out before we move on is the direct link to your Goodreads page. It is one of the first things you see on this page, labeled "URL." When you are adding a Goodreads Follow icon to your blog, this is where you will find the URL to use.

12

PRIMARY AND SECONDARY ACTIVITIES

Before we move on to talk about an author profile, I want to cover what I consider to be the primary and secondary activities of Goodreads. I feel the primary activity on Goodreads is centered around the shelf/review functionality. The secondary activity is to make friends – to network. As an author, the whole reason for being on Goodreads is to network. Because of this, understanding the advantages of various types of connections with other readers is important. Both of these activities are covered in screencasts from the associated course as well as in sections below.

Primary Activity – Shelves/reviews

When you were setting up your "Personal" account, you got a taste of the shelves Goodreads has when you were asked if you "Want to Read" some of the books you were shown. If you clicked on the button, the book would have been put on a "To Read" shelf for you.

Goodreads allows every member with a Personal Profile to create virtual shelves for their books. There are default shelves that every account comes with—"Read," "To-Read" ("Want to Read"), and "Currently Reading." As mentioned previously, the action of adding books to shelves is an action that started during your account signup. I see it as the mark of a true bookworm—the desire to share the books we read.

As I will mention frequently, you should be joining Goodreads as a reader looking to make friends, to network. List some books that you have read, join the discussion of your favorite titles, and put books on shelves. I am suspicious of people who want to be friends with me who have no books on their shelves (or only one—theirs). In my mind, they aren't on Goodreads as readers. They are there to tell me about their book but aren't interested in interacting as a member reader. I don't respond to friend requests for these people.

I LOVE the ability to add books to my virtual shelves. As I've mentioned before, I used to be that person who went book shopping with a binder full of lists of books I was looking for and books I have read. I now have the Goodreads app on my phone and a shelf called "To Purchase." When I go book shopping, I just need to take my phone with me! Huge improvement in my mind!

Let's talk about shelves. As mentioned above, every account holder gets three shelves when they open their account—"Read," "To-Read" (or "Want to Read" as it is labeled in some areas), and "Currently Reading," but you can create shelves as needed. Although as a reader, you can put books on whatever shelves you want or choose to create, as an author you want readers to put your book on one of the preset shelves, as it will then be shown on the Newsfeed for every one of their friends to see. It will also affect Goodreads' algorithm. This is a little bit of free advertising and for the bookworm the potential for Goodreads recommendations.

According to the experts on the functionality of the Goodreads' algorithm, books being put on shelves is more important than your book being reviewed or receiving stars. The Goodreads algorithm pays attention to how many times your book is placed on shelves. Authors would like readers to mark their book as "To read" for that purpose. The more your book shows up on the "To Read" shelves, the higher it will show on the "Popular Books." We will discuss further in the chapter on the "Explore" section of Goodreads.

If you remember at the beginning of the book, I mentioned the "My Books" button on the menu bar that so many find misleading. This button is used to bring us to the page that shows the books we have entered onto shelves.

Walk with me and click on your "My Books" link and you will be taken to a page with a list of books that occupies the right 75% of the screen and a list of shelves on the left 25%.

Let's assume you have added some books. You can sort them on to shelves, either the shelves that Goodreads provides you with, or you can use the "Add Shelf" link and create some custom ones for yourself. Put your stamp on the choice of shelves. As I've mentioned, I have one called "To Purchase," but I have other shelves for other purposes.

It is possible to independently add shelves and then add books to these shelves. Books can be added to multiple shelves.

Let's look at the right section of the screen and do a quick tour of the information that is available. Along the top, you will see buttons that will allow you to alter the settings, as well as change the display from a list to more of a grid arrangement. Regardless of how you prefer your collection of books to be displayed if you hover your mouse over the cover graphic, you will get a popup that displays the blurb of the book, the star ratings, and the shelf you have placed that book on.

If you have your books displayed as a list, the shelves are visible as one of the columns of information.

Each book record that exists in your list of books, has information associated with it. You should see a cover graphic, title, and subtitle, author, average rating, rating, shelves, date read, and date added. To the far right is an X, which will allow you to delete the listing. To add each book to a shelf, click on the edit link in the shelves column and choose from the shelves listed or create one on the fly. Organize your books and give a boost to some of your favorite authors!

If you are feeling adventurous, find some more books to put on shelves—your fellow authors' books, perhaps. If you look above the listing of books you will see the "Search and Add Books" field. The search field will allow you to search using the Title, Author, or ISBN. Use this to find the book you are currently reading, or maybe one you are hoping to read. Add it to a shelf and practice this action. Not only will you be helping out another author, but you will be helping yourself understand another part of Goodreads.

There is more to the "Books" area than just shelves. If you look at the upper menu area, beside the field used to find some new books, you will see "Batch Edit," "Settings" (which allows you to change the view of what you see), and 'Print.'

Looking to the left of your list of books and under your list of shelves, you can see what is labeled 'Tools" and "Add Books." Looking at the links there you have access to Recommendations, add an Amazon book purchase, widgets (these would be reader widgets), Import/Export (allowing you to import or export a list of books) & find duplicates.

Although many of these choices are available in several different areas of the Goodreads website (and we will talk about many of them in later sections), click on a selection of the links now and see where they lead. We have already talked about reader widgets and mentioned recommendations, but some of the other bells and whistles are entertaining.

Secondary Activity – Friends/Followers/Favorites

When I wrote the original version of this book, Goodreads offered two types of connections between people. You could be a friend of someone, or you could be a fan of an author. Simple. Several years ago, Goodreads changed this model and created Friends/Followers/Favorites. This change was quietly snuck in and took quite a few people by surprise—me included! I went from having 90 fans to having over 3000, the same number as I had friends, overnight.

When I went searching for an explanation, I did find that Goodreads had announced this in one of their groups.

Let's define the groups:

Follower: A person who "follows" an author will receive the author's updates on their Newsfeed. This will include their blog posts. This is an automatic status based on a request from a reader and doesn't require the author to approve (similar to the previous "fan" status).

Friend: A friend status is something that has to be approved by the receiving party and is capped at 5000 according to Goodreads (although I know people who have surpassed this supposed cap). This ability is somewhat hidden because one has to click on a drop-down menu to see this choice. This functionality is the only status that didn't change when Goodreads reorganized.

Favorite: The status of Favorite is something readers can add to any author they follow. It doesn't seem to give any special powers, but it is described in the Goodreads "Help" documents as something readers can show off on their profile. When I went looking for my Favorite Authors, I found the section near the bottom of my reader profile, not nearly as visible as I was anticipating from the description.

A common question people ask who are just learning to navigate Goodreads is where are the buttons or links that control the friend/follow/favorite functionality. To find them, go to your Goodreads account, and in the search box, type in the name of your favorite author. Once the author's profile page is in front of you, you should be able to see the "Follow Author" button under their profile picture. For the other choices, click on the down arrow to the right of this button and you should see the choices for friend and favorite as well as several other selections.

If you bring up the profile for a reader, the page will look quite different. The button allowing you to add them as a friend and follow their reviews is under the box of their profile information.

As far as you, the author, is concerned, you want to get as many "Friends" as well as "Followers" as you can. Let's start with why followers? There are two main reasons for this. First of all, the number of followers is not capped, and secondly, followers are notified of new blog posts and new book releases. Remember, you want to be able to network and communicate with readers, so you want them to have access to your blog posts and new release notifications. This isn't an easy task, however, as the reader needs to initiate this action. It isn't something that you can start and they just need to confirm. Encouraging readers to "follow" you in the back matter of your books & blog posts can be very successful.

Friends are useful also but in different ways. You can send event invites to them (but not to followers) for example. A note of caution: since the number of friends you can have on Goodreads is capped at 5000, choose carefully. Although 5000 may seem like a large number initially, it is still a limit. Focus your friend requests on readers, not authors, and specifically readers of the genre you write. Remember, you are here as a reader, but also to network with a community you create. Although fellow authors may be very supportive of your work, you need to focus on readers first.

Since we have to approve friendships on Goodreads, it stands to reason that we can "Unfriend" also. To find a list of friends, click on your picture on the upper right of the list and click on "Friends." This will show you a sortable list of your friends. Click on the "Edit Friends" link in the upper right and you can click on the X to un-friend (the person will not be notified if you un-friend them). You will see that you have quite a bit of information about your friends from this list—how many books they have shelved, what they are reading, and how many other friends they have. You can also use the search field to search your list of friends for someone in particular.

How many friends/followers do you have? Do you know where to look to find out? As you will find out, the numbers and details can be found in several places.

13

AUTHOR PROFILE

Claim your Status

Now that you have a Personal profile set up, let's look at creating your Author Profile. As was mentioned previously, Goodreads offers authors the ability to create a special profile and claim their books. This profile comes complete with several special abilities. The course associated with this book has a screencast associated with this chapter.

It is only possible to claim your author status if your book is already published or in preorder. To see if your book is in the Goodreads system, go up to the search field and enter the title of your book and search. If found, click on the entry and scroll down looking for a link that says, "Is this you? Let us know." Clicking on this link will send a message to Goodreads to start the process of authorizing your author status. When authorized, you will receive an email with instructions on setting up your author profile.

If you have already claimed your author status, let's get busy filling out all the information you need to create a robust author presence!

Author Profile

There are several ways to access your author information. Hover over your profile picture in the upper right and choose "View Profile." If your author status has been assigned, you should see a profile with the title of "Goodreads Author" in the upper right. You should also see "Edit Author Profile" just to the right of your name. Click on that link to get to the page where you can edit this content. You can also get to the same place by clicking on the second entry after you click on your photo in the upper right—"Author Dashboard." Then click on "Edit My Author Profile." Lastly, you can get there by clicking on "Account Settings"—also under your photo in the upper right corner.

However you get to the correct point, work your way down the page filling in as much as you are comfortable doing. You'll notice that the information is very similar to what you entered as a reader. What I find interesting is that now you have author status, the system will preferentially pick up your author information, not your reader information. As you will see as we go on however, there will be bits and pieces of your reader information still active and found various places.

Once you have completed the information on the left, make sure you upload an author photo (or several if you want). At this point, I encourage you to go to the bottom left of the page and click on save before you go any further.

If you look just underneath where your photo sits, you can see links to where you can upload a video, view any upcoming events you have created, edit your blog, and create an author widget. We will get to all of these things in turn, but to start, we need to proof the information that has just been entered. To do that, click on the "View Your Dashboard" text link.

14

ATTACH YOUR BOOK(S) TO YOUR PROFILE

The next step is to make sure your published titles are attached to your Author Profile. Although the steps are covered below, you can also view a screencast of the process in the course associated with this book. If you are just starting with Goodreads and you have just claimed your one book, this information may not be necessary. In my experience, if you get help from Goodreads to claim your first book, the rest of the books you publish just seem to automatically attach themselves to your profile as an author. However, there are periodically glitches in the system.

If you are an author with books that have been published for some time (and available on Amazon), I would be surprised if the books are not on Goodreads. That being said, if you search for your books and can't find them, you will need to add them manually.

Let's start from the beginning and go through this process one step at a time.

The first step is to check to see if your books have already been associated with you. Click on Home and then click on your picture in the upper right, and then choose "Author Dashboard" from the dropdown menu. Underneath the stats area, you should see a section labeled "Your Books." If all your books are listed there, you don't need to manually add them, but I would suggest going through the listing(s) to check the content.

If you need to attach a book, the first step is to go to the top of the page and look for the search field. It allows a search by Title/Author/ISBN. I would suggest you search by title or ISBN. If you find your title, then just go ahead and claim it. If you don't see your title, you will enter it manually. You do that by clicking on the "Add A Book" link to the right of the "Your Books" label.

Clicking on the "Add a Book" will bring up an information screen that will allow you to fill in the details of your book. Fill in the form completely. There is a "Guidelines" box on the right-hand side of your screen to find help if you have any questions about some of the fields. Remember to add your cover image by using the button in the upper right-hand corner, When you are finished, click "Save" at the bottom of the page. Lastly, you are encouraged to put the book on a shelf and then click on "Save."

If you return to your "Author Dashboard," you should see your book in place. Make sure you click on it and proof your entry.

15

AUTHOR DASHBOARD

To find the "Author Dashboard" click on the "Home" link on the far left, then move to the right and click on your picture. From the dropdown menu choose "Author Dashboard" to open that page. Let's take a tour of the location of all the specialized areas, and then we will talk about them one by one. There is a screencast as part of the course associated with this book that is associated with this chapter.

Starting in the upper left is your author photo beside the snapshot of stats that Goodreads provides for authors. Underneath that is a list of the author's books (labeled "Your Books") each with a little snapshot of information. Below the "Your Books" section is new functionality for Goodreads—the "Ask an Author" area. Below this is the "Your Blog" section, followed by "Advertise your Book" and "Your Giveaways." The last item on the left side is "E-books."

Moving to the right side of the "Author Dashboard," at the top are several direct links to commonly used functions. Below that is a snippet look at the "Authors & Advertisers Blog," "Author Tutorial," and "Author Widgets," and finally "Followers."

In the next few sections, we are going to gradually work our way through this page of "Author" functions.

. . .

Stats

I like to refer to this area as a snapshot of the health of your Goodreads account both "you" as a reader as well as "you" as an author. At the top of the box under your name is your overall rating in stars and the total number of ratings. Under that title line, there are two columns of information. Because of this display, I can quickly see ten pieces of information as follows:

• Number of works (published works by you)

• Total books added (to shelves of the books you have written)

• Total Ratings (giving a book a number out of 5 for books you have written)

• Total Reviews (text comments on a book you have written)

• On To-Read Shelf (number of books of yours on others' To-Read shelf)

• Added by Unique Users (books you have written that have been added to shelves by unique Goodreads members)

• Followers (number of followers)

• Friends (number of friends)

• Books I've added (to custom shelves as a reader)

• Books I've reviewed (text reviews as a reader)

I like the concise nature of the collection of information, but authors are frequently confused by the combination of author and reader stats. Below this box is a prompt to "View Recent Work Stats." This will show you how many and when your books have been added to shelves. I don't find the Work Stats all that helpful, but have a look and see if you have any interest in this information.

Your Books (not to be confused with My Books – an entry in the upper menu bar)

The "Your Books" section will display the books that you have published, each with a little snapshot of its stats. Only six books show at a time. If you have published more than six books, you will have to find the "Next" link at the bottom right of this area to see the rest of your books.

Each book title/cover graphic can be clicked onto see the "Book detail" page. From that point, you can see the "Add Preview" or "View Excerpt" link on the left, a selection of stats about the book, the book's blurb, and at the bottom of this segment, the ability to edit all these details.

Just to remind you, at this point, you are seeing the kind of detail readers can see when they look at this view. The reader gets the title, tagline, author, and cover graphic. You can see a star representation of this book's overall rating, the number of ratings this book has, and how many reviews. You can also click on the 'Ratings Details' link and that will bring up a pop-up screen that summarizes the ratings.

Moving further down the page, you can see the blurb of the book as well as the publisher, info, other publishing details, and lastly, the various covers or editions. All of this information can be changed using the "Edit Details" link at the bottom right of this area. Although in most cases, the information about your book is pulled from its Amazon listing, you will want to look over each book's listing and make sure everything is correct. If something needs tweaking, use the edit button and change as needed.

Below this section is the area that lists the reviews. You'll notice that reviews are divided up into Friend Reviews, Reviews from People You Follow, and Community Reviews. Before you get to Community Reviews, you will likely see if your book is on a Listopia list and any questions you may have answered regarding this book in the Author Q&A section. Reviews with text are shown before the reviews that only contain a star rating.

At the very bottom of the page is a section labeled "Discuss This Book." If any discussions have been started about this book, you can monitor them or chime in. As in other areas of the book, I mention that Goodreads is a site for readers; authors need to tread lightly. Readers may start up a discussion about your book that doesn't need to involve you. Be careful what you say.

• • •

Ask the Author

The "Ask the Author" section is a somewhat new offering from Goodreads. Goodreads has created a selection of six fairly common questions. Readers can add a question and the author is then notified that there is a question to answer. The author also can create a customized greeting message to their readers. This whole section can be turned on or off and authors can choose to get a daily email or a digest of questions. I've never had anyone ask me a question in this section, but when I look at this area for several of my favorite authors, they have answered quite a few questions.

It is suggested by Goodreads that you answer the basic questions they offer and see if you are asked any other questions. Honestly, when this first appeared on my "Author Dashboard," I wasn't impressed. I've been won over, however, and I understand how this can allow authors to communicate easily with readers and win over some fans. It's like breaking the ice at a party. If you answer the initial questions, your readers will see that you are communicative, friendly, and willing to share with them. In this time of easy access to authors by readers, this is yet another point at which authors can demonstrate how friendly they are.

Your Blog

Goodreads offers authors the ability to have two types of blog posts. It allows all authors to have their personal blog's posts automatically feed into their Goodreads author account and show under the "Your Blog" label on the Author Dashboard. It also allows authors to create blog posts that are independent of their actual blogs. Both of these types of blog posts are available for readers to view and comment on.

The fact that your blog posts can show on your "Author Dashboard" and be shown to Goodreads' members is a big deal! What makes it even more special is that anyone who is a follower of yours will be notified as part of their emailed notifications, as well as appearing on their Newsfeed when you post a new blog post. In addition to it being visible to anyone looking at your author profile, readers can subscribe to your blog through Goodreads. I was amazed to see that I have 293 subscribers to this blog feed. It may not seem like a lot in the big picture, but I see it as 293 subscribers that I might not otherwise have had.

It is just another way to connect with readers that is free. As I'm fond of saying, we need to create interesting content on our blogs and social media and allow our readers to access that information and interact with us in whatever way is convenient to them, not to us.

The other type of blog posts that Goodreads allows for is a post that is created on Goodreads and will appear as part of your list of blog posts but will not appear on your actual blog. After clicking on "Your Blog" to see the details of the blog posts coming from your actual blog, look to the right and you will see a "New Post" text link. If you click on that, you will see the "New Blog Post" screen appear. To the right of the Title and Body fields is a box with the label of "Formatting Tips"—a list of HTML tags you can use to format this blog post.

This little addition to your ability to communicate with your Goodreads reader gives you the ability to pass on information to just people who connect with you there. They will see this note on their Newsfeed as well as be notified by an email notification that you have created this post. Many readers see this type of communication to be less intrusive than the event system, which we will talk about in chapter 20.

Advertise Your Book

Moving further down the author dashboard page you will see that Goodreads offers authors several choices of Advertising. The quote from this section reads:

> *With over 300 million page views and 45 million unique visitors a month, Goodreads offers integrated advertising and book launch packages designed to target and reach readers.*

Although I used to enjoy the self-serve advertising that Goodreads offered, they have recently removed that function. They now focus on their higher-end advertising products. They will carry out targeted direct advertising and strategic launch programs. As of this writing, there are no prices available on the website, but it is my understanding this advertising has a large price tag. We won't be covering the details of this sort of advertising in this book.

Your Giveaways

The next section that you will see on your "Author Dashboard" is titled "Your Giveaways." If you have offered Giveaways in the past, you will see them listed below the "Your Giveaways" heading along with some details of that event.

> **As is stated on the site,** *"Listing a giveaway is a great way to get exposure for your book. You can list any of your pre-release or published books for a giveaway, regardless of publication date."*

This section of the author dashboard is meant to be "display" only. Even when you click on the title, you are only led to a display area. I will walk through setting up a new giveaway in Chapter 20.

EBooks

The next section that we come to is labeled "E-books." There are two sections on Goodreads that are labeled E-books. This section refers to a short excerpt from your book(s) that you upload to be viewed by readers.

As I'm sure you know, a writing sample is the best friend of a new author. Most retailers allow readers to sample a book.

The sample is called an "ebook," "excerpt," or "preview" at various places on Goodreads. Initially, Goodreads allowed authors to upload a sample of their work that readers could then view. They have removed that functionality for the most part and are relying on the "Preview" functionality or the "Look Inside" functionality coming from Amazon's KDP.

Make sure that there is a "Preview" link showing on your book detail page. As I've said previously, I feel we should take advantage of as many of the perks they offer as is logical. Book buyers are methodical people. They take a great deal of time and care in their purchase. Provide potential buyers of your book as much help as they need to make a purchase decision.

Authors & Advertiser's Blog

The "Authors & Advertiser's Blog" is the next section we will talk about. When I wrote the original version of this book, there were eleven blog posts available. At the time of this writing, there are quite a few posts and they seem to be appearing on a more regular basis. I'm not sure what Goodreads' intent is with this blog. I notice several of the posts on the blog are included as part of my Author newsletter that arrives in my inbox. I encourage you to read some of the posts. There is quite an eclectic collection of information, but they are quite interesting!

If this type of information is interesting to you, you can subscribe to the feed and have the opportunity to read the posts when they come out.

Author Tutorial

Below the "Authors & Advertiser's blog" section you will find a section called "Author Tutorial." If you click on the "Read the Tutorial" link, you will be taken to a series of simple tutorials designed to help the author new to Goodreads. There isn't a huge amount of information to overwhelm, but there are a few tips and tricks that are not necessarily intuitive.

One link I will point out to you from this page is the "View All Goodreads Authors" link. At the time of this writing, Goodreads has 301,332 authors. It is possible to see a list of all Goodreads authors and even sort the list in a variety of ways. I found it very interesting to see that Stephen King was listed as the most popular author with 723,673 followers to date.

Author Widgets

Although we have mentioned reader widgets in the first section of this book, I'm very fond of the author's widgets that Goodreads offers. If you click on the "Add the Author Widget" link, you will be brought to a page that displays all of the various types of widgets it supports. Widgets range from the plain follow link to much more complicated collections of information. Goodreads author widgets are great fun to play with. Both reader and author widgets are discussed in one of the screencasts available in the course associated with this book.

For those of you who are beginners with your blogs, a widget is something that is typically put on the sidebar of your blog, within the text of a post, or possibly the footer to display information. What Goodreads offers you is the ability to customize some information that you want to display and provides the code that you can copy and paste into place to display it. I have created YouTube videos that help you with the blog side of this project. Look for links to the videos at the end of this book. Let's talk about a couple of my favorite widgets from the Author grouping.

As you scan through the widget choices available, I'm sure you'll see some that pique your interest. My two favorite widgets are the Review widget and the Books Widget. The Review widget allows you to choose one of your books and display a selected number of reviews for that book. When you click on the "Configure & add widget" button, you find that you will be allowed to select a large number of things about your widget, from height and width to the color of links. Goodreads allows quite a bit of customization to occur.

Once you are finished entering info, click on the submit button and then copy the code to a text widget or gadget on your blog.

Similarly, the Books Widget allows you to display a selection of books on the sidebar of your blog. You are encouraged to choose the number of books to be displayed and can see a sample of the information that will be shown. As before, you copy the offered code and paste it into a text widget/gadget on the sidebar of your blog or into the Text side of your blog post.

Followers

The last section that we come to as we look at the right-hand side of the "Author Dashboard" is Followers. You might be asking yourself, "Why are only the followers displayed in this area?" The short answer is that followers are considered to be the most important relationship for authors. If you click on the "More Followers" link at the bottom of this section, you will see a column arrangement of your followers along with information on what book they are currently reading (if they have entered that information) along with whether or not you friend them, or follow their reviews. If someone who follows you is an author, you will be offered the chance to follow them as well.

As I'm sure you are remembering, the subject of friends/followers/favorites was covered in more detail in chapter 11.

16

SUMMARY OF THE AUTHOR PROFILE

Direct your attention to the upper right where you should now see a picture/Gravatar and click on it. Let's take a quick peek at the menu items that are available there.

You will see the following on the menu:

- Profile
- Author Dashboard (only present once you have received author status)
- Friends
- Groups
- Discussions
- Comments
- Reading Challenge
- Kindle Notes & Highlights
- Quotes
- Favorite Genres
- Friends' Recommendations
- Account Settings
- Help

- Sign Out

Let's briefly discuss each of these menu items.

Profile – As we've seen in previous sections, this shortcut will take you to your "Personal" profile if you don't yet have author status or your Author Profile if you do.

Author Dashboard – Again, as we've seen in previous sections, this link will take you directly to your Author Dashboard. This is considered to be the go-to overview of you (as an author), your books, and your various author functionalities as we discussed in the previous chapter.

Friends – This shortcut will take you to what I call the "Friend's dashboard." We discussed this further in chapter 11.

Groups – This shortcut will take you to a summary page of your group activities, both invitations you may have received to join groups and summaries of groups that you have joined.

Discussions – This shortcut will take you to another summary page that will allow you to see and respond to either book discussions or group discussions.

Comments – This link is handy as it takes you to a page that shows a summary of comments, either a comment you have made or others have left for you. There are many opportunities to leave comments, so having this summary page is useful as all the comments can be seen and responded to in one location.

Comments can be left almost anywhere. Goodreads allows you to comment on reviews. If you look at the bottom of a review for your book, or any book, you will see you have the ability to comment or to like. Both of these functions allow you to show a response, but the comment allows you to use words for your response.

Comments can also be left on blog posts. These comments are not very visible, in my opinion, but if you are the author of the blog post, you will be notified of the comment. Lastly, comments can also be left on Events.

Remember to treat other readers as you would like to be treated yourself. Leaving thoughtless comments is not appreciated and may result in an unnecessary flame war.

Reading Challenge – I love this shortcut! If you have joined a Reading Challenge (and I highly suggest that you do), this link will bring you to a summary page of your Reading Challenge. We discuss Reading Challenges several times in this book. It is one of the first actions you take when creating a new account.

Kindle Notes & Highlights - If you have attached your Amazon account to your Goodreads account it will display the Kindle books that you have purchased from Amazon. Each listing has a summary of the notes and highlights you have added to each book. It is an interesting section. If adding notes is something that you like to do, this is the only place I'm aware of that you can see a summary of all these notations.

Quotes – This link will take you to the page that shows quotes you have created or quotes that you have "liked." We will talk again about quotes in a future chapter.

. . .

Favorite Genres – This link takes you to a page that allows you to fine-tune your choices for favorite genres. As we've talked about in previous chapters and will discuss again in the future, being a reader on Goodreads is important. Choosing Favorite Genres is at the backbone of the recommendation system that I'm so fond of.

Friends' Recommendations – This short cut leads you to a summary page of all recommendations. We'll talk more about recommendations in a future chapter.

Account Settings – We have looked at this shortcut previously. It leads to the edit page for your basic author information.

Help – This shortcut is one to keep in mind. Although Goodreads can be a challenging site to navigate, they have a fairly well-organized help section. You can also contact them directly. I have found them to be quite responsive when I have submitted questions.

Sign Out – Although many people just leave themselves logged onto Goodreads, the paranoid part of me would like to remind you to log out of your Goodreads account when you leave. Don't just shut down the browser window.

17

ADDITIONAL FUNCTIONALITIES

Tags and Keywords

Tags and Keywords are used liberally on Goodreads. Generally speaking, tags are single words or short phrases that are used to describe something. Keywords are often limited to a single important or all-encompassing descriptive word or phrase. This is not true on Goodreads. In some places, Goodreads asks for Keywords and in others, it asks for Tags. As far as I can figure, Keywords and Tags are used interchangeably on this site. When entering a review, you are given the choice of Tags/Bookshelf. This allows you to choose the bookshelf you have associated this book with as well as tags that will allow readers to find your review by searching tags/keywords.

To play with this function, enter your favorite keyword/tag in various search fields and see what comes up. I played for a while using the Tag of "Romance" and in some locations, the word romance had to be in the search result. In other locations, the word "Romance" seemed to be a true tag that someone had entered. As we go forward in our description of the various functionalities of Goodreads, you will see how frequently you have the opportunity to use Tags and Keywords. You will also see how inconsistently they are applied. Treat Tags and Keywords as the same—a word or a small phrase that can be used to describe an item and bring searchers to it.

Videos and Book Trailers

One last extra function that we need to talk about is a much-overlooked author function. Authors can add videos or book trailers to their author profile. You can get to this area in two ways, either by clicking on your picture in the upper right and then clicking on "View Profile" and then "Edit Author Profile" or clicking on your picture in the upper right and then click on "Account Settings." If your starting point is "Profile," you should see the video prompt below your photo on the left. If your starting point is "Account Settings," look below your profile picture on the right and you will see the label of Videos and the "Add New" link on the right end of this banner. Although you can't upload a video file, you can attach a link to a video that is held elsewhere—the accepted hosting sites are currently YouTube and Livestream.

Once the link and the title are entered in the form, you can enter a description and choose a book this video is about. Videos need not be limited to book trailers. For example, I have instructional videos about technical subjects posted on YouTube, and they can also be viewed from my Goodreads account. Authors will also upload little clips from book signings or conferences. I'm sure there is a limit to the number of videos that can be displayed in this area, but I haven't hit it yet.

18

BOOKS AND SHELVES

My Books

The next menu item we will look at is "My Books." As I've mentioned in previous chapters, often a point of confusion as the label of "My Books" refers to books you have put on shelves and indicated an interest in reading. The "Your Books" label, which we find as part of our Author Dashboard, refers to the books you have published.

Click on the "My Books" link and you will bring up a screen we looked at in a previous chapter. I feel it is important to be a reader first and an author second. Goodreads was built as a site for readers, not authors. In my opinion, some of the friction that occurs between readers and authors occurs when authors forget that they are readers, too. I know you all read books! I also know you have a book or some books you have written that you want to sell. So do I. But on Goodreads, leave your author hat at home and be a book lover.

One of the ways you can be a book lover is to use the "My Books" section. List some of the books you have read. Remember that listing a book on a shelf helps the author of that book according to the Goodreads algorithms. If you belong to a critique group, add all your fellow authors' published books to a "Read" or "To Be Read" shelf. This will help your friends. Do you have an author whom you haven't met personally but admire their work? Add their books to your "Read" or "To Read" shelf. Help them out so they keep writing books you like!

Shelves

Although you may limit yourself to the preset shelves, try to be adventurous and add a few custom shelves. Readers choose to have different shelves for different reasons. I have a shelf that lists all the books that I have on my TBR pile (which in reality is multiple boxes in my closet). I feel a sense of achievement when I take a book off that shelf! I also have a shelf that lists all the books I want to purchase. I frequently stumble on a new author or a series, and I want to keep track of books I'm looking for, especially books from new-to-me authors with extensive back-lists. As I mentioned in one of the first chapters of this book, I simply love the mobile app of Goodreads. You see...I read on a very tight budget. I either find books in the library or used bookstores. I rarely buy books new, especially in Canada, where a new paperback is too expensive. Gone are the days when I would walk into my favorite bookstore clutching my overstuffed binder containing my lists of books I was looking for. I can now discreetly scan the shelves with my iPhone in hand and my 'to-purchase' shelf loaded on my app.

Have I convinced you to try out the shelving system yet?

Other than the shelf functionality, take a quick peek at the information available to you at a glance regarding the books you have entered. You can see the title, the author's name, the average rating along with the rating that you gave it if you did, the shelf or shelves that you put the book on, the date you read it, as well as adding it to the system. You also can edit the listing, edit the shelf/shelves, and lastly, you can simply delete the listing altogether.

Keeping with the theme of seeing Goodreads as a "Reader Heaven," let's talk about the ability to assign ratings and reviews to books. As was pointed out in a seminar I recently attended, if you have thin skin and it upsets you to look at reviews or ratings of your books, don't. Readers have the right to say whatever they want about books, provided they aren't vindictive or threatening. Remember, as an artist, you are trying to provoke a response with your book. Bad reviews don't ruin a career; bad manners and bad editing can, however. Case in point: look at the reviews of some of literature's greats, look at the reviews for million sellers. They aren't all 5 stars, yet they have sold, and continue to sell millions.

Goodreads allows readers to assign ratings and reviews to books. A rating is simply some stars out of 5. A review is a text response for the book in addition to, or in exclusion of, the number of stars. In other words, it is possible to leave a text review and not assign a rating, and it is possible to leave a star rating without leaving a text statement of any sort.

As an author, I appreciate both kinds of responses to my books. I must admit, if the stars are lower, I'd like to know what was disappointing to the reader because I'm always seeking to improve. Nonetheless, I appreciate the time that anyone takes to share their thoughts with me.

As a reader, I frequently leave a starred rating, but not much in terms of text, as I like to review on my book blog. When I do leave a text response, I often use that area to help myself remember the book and what's coming next.

What is important on Goodreads is the number of times a book is put on a shelf and to a minor extent, the number of ratings/reviews it gets. Every time someone does something with your book, it goes on that person's news feed and your book cover is shown to all their friends and followers. That's what is important!

. . .

I'll get down off my soapbox and talk about reviews and the functionality around reviews.

Many regard reviews on Goodreads as better or more accurate or more unbiased than those posted anywhere else. For the most part, Goodreads' reviewers do not care if you buy, borrow, or ignore the book because they just enjoy reading and sharing their thoughts.

Let's look at the reviews for a book that you have read. Choose a book and click on it to bring up the book's record.

Sorting Reviews

Reviews can be sorted according to various criteria. Although Goodreads encourages you to read your friends' reviews first, if you scroll down, you will find a section labeled "Community Reviews," listing reviews from people who are not your friends.

There are two ways of sorting the "Community" reviews for a book. They can be filtered by the number of stars or the edition numbers, they can be sorted by default, from the newest to oldest, or from the oldest to newest. Or you can simply click on "Rating Detail" and see a summary of the ratings from everyone who has rated the book in a lovely bar graph.

Use the record for your favorite book and play with the sorting system. Become familiar with it.

One last comment about reviews: the only possible response to one, either a good one or a bad one is 'Thank you for reading my book." There is absolutely nothing to be gained from going after the reviewer on any forum, be it Goodreads or Amazon, or anywhere else. You should not retaliate under any circumstances. Trolls will come out to play and that is never a good thing.

19

BROWSE MENU

In this next section, we are going to talk about all of the items listed on the Browse menu. As I said at the beginning of the book, Goodreads is continually carrying out reorganizations. In the most recent reorganization, they put most of the functionality into groups. The Browse section is for the voracious reader—it's all about finding books and celebrating authors. The items included in this menu are:

- Recommendations
- Choice Awards
- Giveaways
- New Releases
- Lists
- News & Interviews

Recommendations

As I've mentioned before, the recommendations from Goodreads is one of my favorite parts of the site's functionality. I read a lot of books, and I'm often on the lookout for a new author to read, or a new book that has been released. Goodreads uses a combination of the books you have indicated an interest in reading, the books you have shelved, as well as your response to their suggestions, to plug into their algorithms and fine-tune their recommendations to you.

Let's look at your Recommendations page. Everyone's page will look a bit different as everyone will have a slightly different selection of books indicated as wanting to read, or placed on shelves. Generally speaking, you will be offered recommendations based on books on various shelves. If you hover your mouse over the cover graphic for a book, you will get a pop-up window which will give you a short blurb for the book and also a reason why this book was suggested to you.

My recommendations are lined up based on my bookshelves. I'm offered five suggestions based on each shelf. Below each book cover is the ability to click on "Want to Read" or a "Not Interested" link. Have a look at each selection and make the appropriate choice. This will help Goodreads get better at suggesting books that you would likely be interested in. I know the suggestions I receive frequently have me heading to Amazon to do some one-clicking!

Looking at the right side of the Recommendations page, you will see that in addition to getting recommendations by shelf, you can also get book suggestions based on some of the genres you read. Below that section, are four more links in the "More Actions" section. They are self-explanatory from their titles. I find that although you can "Give Recommendations" using the appropriate link, this should be used sparingly. Some authors seem to think that recommending their book to everyone on their "Friends" list is a good idea, I see it as the actions of an author interested in the "Buy my Book" type of marketing, not the author who is truly trying to be helpful. Have I recommended one of my books to some of my friends? Yes, but only a few, and only for specific reasons. Am I likely to recommend a romance that I've just finished reading to all my romance book blogger friends on Goodreads? Absolutely! It's nice that people read my reviews on my blog, but every so often I finish a book and think WOW...I need others to read this right now, and I use this system on Goodreads to get a fast message across.

As I've mentioned before, one of the main points you need to be aware of on Goodreads, as well as all other social media sites, is that being blatantly self-promotional all the time you will be tuned out by most users. Because of this, I wouldn't recommend *your* book to everyone who friends you. This should be part of a larger communication strategy.

Let's talk about Goodreads' algorithms for a second. The average public member doesn't ***actually*** know the secrets of Google, Amazon, or Goodreads' algorithms, but experts speculate based on actions that they witness. They take educated guesses. We know from actions on Goodreads (as well as thoughts from people smarter than me) that various actions will push books higher in the Goodreads rankings. Actions like putting books on shelves, ranking, and rating books will push a book higher and higher in the algorithms. For this reason, we want to encourage these behaviors. We can do this in various ways, from putting books on shelves to using widgets that encourage this on our blogs.

Choice Awards

Every year Goodreads offers readers the chance to vote on their favorite book or books of the year. Goodreads uses their statistics to choose the top fifteen books in every genre and allows several rounds of voting. The first round of voting takes the list of fifteen books to ten books, and then the next round of voting takes the number to five, and in the third round of voting, one book is chosen. The book needs to be published in the previous year (November to November) that the contest is held in, and an author can be nominated for multiple books and in multiple categories or genres.

If you have been a member of Goodreads for a while, you will realize that requests to vote for a Choice Award start flying around the beginning of November each year. Even though Goodreads chooses the original fifteen books, readers vote for and choose the winners.

Although it is difficult to be one of the top books in your genre, the prestige is huge! Some authors work towards this award all year—hence the encouragement for reviews/ratings/shelves!

. . .

Giveaways

"Giveaways" is an area of Goodreads that seems to be continually in a state of change. It has gone from one of my most favorite functionalities to a paid function that is out of my price range.

Goodreads offers the ability for authors to list paperback books and Kindle books for a random giveaway.

Generally speaking, you enter the ISBN of the paperback version of your book, enter a short blurb, and choose the length of time the giveaway is available. You then control who can enter the giveaway by choosing which countries the giveaway is active for.

Let's talk specifics about the strategies and set up.

Posting a giveaway is easy. From the Giveaway page, choose "List a Giveaway" on the right, and you will be presented with the choice of Kindle or print. Pick one and then you are asked if you are the publisher or author. Pick one of those two and then you are presented with the choice of Standard ($119) or Premium ($599). Once that choice is made, you will be lead through the details of creating the entry.

Choose the date range that you want, (a month is what is suggested), and the ISBN for the book. If your book hasn't been released yet, enter the release date and then choose the country(s). Choose the number of books that you have decided to give away followed by a blurb. This isn't necessarily the official blurb for the book; it is a sales pitch. Encourage people to enter your giveaway! At the end of the form, you need to acknowledge the terms and conditions set out by Goodreads. The last and very important step… you need to respond to the email confirmation notice for your giveaway to appear. This step is very important. If you don't respond to the email, the giveaway will never go live.

Studies indicate that to optimize the buzz for your book, a Goodreads Giveaway is a good addition to add this buzz. With the switch to this being a paid functionality, the jury is still out on not only how popular the giveaways continue to be but also how many authors can afford this perk. Goodreads claims the average giveaway attracts 825 entries and that more than 400,000 people enter them daily.

New Releases

"New Releases" is a great page for readers of all stripes! This is where you can find out about the new releases from authors you follow. As an author, this page will help you attract attention to your latest release. As a reader, this is a great place to find new books and also find out about new releases from your favorite author.

The main portion of this page will list the current month's new releases for "My Authors" or authors for whom you have shelved previous books or authors you follow, as well as by genre, but there is a lot more information than that. Off to the right is a series of short cuts.

You can change your new releases mailer preferences, edit your genre preferences, and edit your email preferences. Below that you can view "Popular New Releases," a group of book covers in a grid, a collection of all sorts of new releases from various genres. I am assuming that this sort of display will allow for the book cover art to attract new readers. At the bottom of the grid is a link to allow you to click and view "More New Releases."

This link leads to a page that will list the top 200 books published in the current month along with a few details about the book and an invitation to click on the "Want to Read" button. This page can be adjusted by month and year, allowing you to view the top 200 of a past date. There is also a series of short cut links to similar functionality.

Lists

Goodreads uses Lists or Listopia, of which everyone, authors as well as readers, should take advantage of. A "List" or "Listopia" (the title is used interchangeably) is simply a list of books usually centered around a certain theme. For example, you can create a list of your favorite Romance Novels set in Regency England released in

2020 (that would be my ideal list). Create your own list and have people vote on the books you've chosen and/or you can vote on other people's lists.

Although some people feel it's a good idea to create a list with your books on it to increase the visibility of your book, I have a slightly different take on the use of Listopia. I like to create lists of books that contain, let's say, a dozen books that include one of my books, but eleven other books that are very similar, and invite people to vote on them. Yes, I am publicizing my book, but I'm also giving a boost to eleven other books as well. I can create similar lists for author group books, critique group books & so on.

To create your own list, go to the Listopia page and look in the upper right for the "Create A List" link. You give the list a title, description, and tags. I feel the tags are really important. If we go back to our previous section on genres, you may have noticed that there are a collection of Listopias that are tagged with the genre. Make sure your Listopia will be found by people who might be interested in these books.

Check back in periodically to see who has voted on your list and if any comments have been added. Find some people who are interested in a similar genre. Not only is it great to have your books added to lists, but these lists have great networking potential with readers!

News & Interviews

As I've mentioned previously, Goodreads has a selection of different ways to communicate information to you. The "News & Interviews" page is one way. It is a display page sharing an assortment of Author Interviews of various authors and various categories/genres of authors, as well as shortcuts to lists of popular books. Much of this information will also appear in the assortment of newsletters that Goodreads sends out. It is a great way to find out about new authors/books and get extra publicity.

20

COMMUNITY LINKS

As I've described previously, all the items grouped under the Community Menu item are functions that have to do with finding friends and networking within the Goodreads system. We'll go through each section one at a time.

Groups

The first entry on the "Community" menu is "Groups." The Groups that exist on Goodreads are the hallmark of the site in many readers' minds. Groups are just what they sound like, a collection of readers with a common interest. Some groups are very active, some not so much, but I guarantee there is a group that will appeal to the reader in you. Case in point: my favorite group "Historical Romance Novels." There's no better place to find out what's new and worth reading or just squee with some fellow readers over our favorite books.

At the time of this writing, there were over 12,700 book clubs with a group on Goodreads. Groups cover every genre, include people from many different countries, and in fact, many groups are not in English. Some groups focus on reading, some focus on writing, and even some groups focus more on social change than actual books.

Let's talk about the groups themselves. Once you click on the word "Groups" you will bring up the main Groups page. You will see that groups are subdivided into sections—Your Groups, Featured Groups, Recently Active Groups, groups reading something from your 'To-Read' shelf, etcetera.

From the main Groups page, click on the title of one that interests you and have a look around. Every group has a title, some graphics to decorate it, and a blurb that describes what the group is about. Every group has moderators/administrators, regular members, a discussion board with possibly many topics. Each group also typically has a list of books, events, possibly videos, and polls. Every group has rules and settings. Usually, the first discussion topic is "rules." Most groups set rules and they WILL enforce the rules. I have found that most active groups have lively discussions about the subject matter at hand. People are free to disagree as long as they are respectful.

To talk about the various functions of a group as well as levels of secrecy that groups can have, let's pretend to create a new group so that you can see not only the information that will be required but also the available choices. You can follow along with this activity on the video as I demonstrate.

From the main Groups page, click on "Create a Group" in the upper right corner. This will bring up the form that needs to be filled in when creating a group. The first three fields which need information are Group Name, Description, and Rules. There is a choice to have the rules shown only to new members, or shown every time someone posts something. In my experience, most groups that I'm familiar with have several sets of rules. There are the overarching rules (which this initial set is usually part of) that describe appropriate behavior and topics of discussion, but the second set is often much more extensive and found as part of the Discussion area. When setting up a group, you must choose a group or book club topic as well as a sub-topic. If you look through the selection, you will see a wide variety of topics! Tags should be added so people looking for a group to join can find your group.

The next section is to choose the degree to which your group is "Public" or what's call the privacy level. As you can see from the choices, the top selection is public. This means the group can be joined by anyone and anyone can view the group information and discussion board even if they aren't a member.

The next level of privacy is "Restricted." This level of privacy allows anyone to see the basic information about the group, but to join, you usually have to have your email address verified and only members can see the discussion boards.

The next level of privacy is labeled "Private." A Private group must have the moderators approve new members and only the moderators can invite new members to the group. Anyone can see the basic information about the group, but only members can see the discussion boards.

The upper level of privacy is called "Secret." In this type of group, new members must be invited and approved by the group's moderators. This type of group will not appear in search results and only group members can see any of the content of the group. The only way you would know about this type of group is if you are invited. It is invisible to Goodreads members.

The last item you need to check is whether your group is for adults. Other than that, you can see that certain powers are decided on for members and moderators as well as the notification frequency that is wanted.

In Goodreads groups, the moderators hold the ultimate power of the operation of the group. They can remove members, delete discussion posts, and add other moderators. In my experience, you don't want to run afoul of a group and their moderators. Join groups as a reader and participate in the discussion. Make friends! Find new books to read, or learn about people who have similar interests, but for heaven's sake, don't go posting your book cover and buy links willy nilly in groups without reading the rules. You don't want to find yourself tossed out on your virtual tushie.

Certain groups are featured by Goodreads, whose editorial staff handpicks those highlighted in the "Featured Groups" category. If you would like to nominate your group to be considered for inclusion, you can apply. Please note that private groups are not eligible.

So, the question is why should you create a group? There are pros and cons to this. One of the pros is that it will, potentially, allow you to interact with a large number of readers. Remember, if you create a group with the sole aim of selling your book, people will recognize this quickly and abandon it. Networking is the thing you should be aiming for, building a community of like-minded readers, not sales.

At the top of the cons list is the amount of time required to promote and moderate a busy group. If you are trying to balance a full-time job, a family, and a writing career, as well as wanting to sleep at night, you might want to consider how much networking you could accomplish with a group. I am not trying to discourage you. I've seen groups done well and the potential is endless.

The next question is should you join some groups? My answer would be absolutely! Join groups that are about topics that you are interested in. If you avoid the obvious "review my book" type of groups, you will find a lot of like-minded readers. In many of these groups, you can post your book cover to advertise it, but the name of the game is networking. To make some friends. You can get involved in some pretty interesting conversations in groups. Take some time and geek out about your favorite subject. Regardless of what it is, I guarantee there is a group of people who share your interests.

Let's face it, readers are not stupid. If they find you interesting and go looking, they can find your books; they're attached to your profile. If they want to buy a book, they know how. Just like at a book signing or an author meet and greet, you chat, make friends, and often book sales come from those networking connections.

Group Widgets

Every group can have a unique widget. Like reader widgets or author widgets, we have discussed in previous chapters, these widgets are easy to create and easy to place on your blog sidebar to advertise your group. To find the Group Widgets, bring up the group you want a widget for.

Partway down the page, you will see a "Group Widget" box. Click on the graphic, and as with the reader widgets and the author widgets, you can customize to a certain extent, then copy the code and paste it into a text widget/gadget on your blog.

Discussions

This area is a relatively new addition to Goodreads and allows account holders to view Group discussions all in one place.

Quotes

Quotes are hugely popular. Quotes are frequently used on social media platforms as a way of stimulating conversation. I know that I have a handful of quotes I often share from some of my favorite books and authors. They get people talking; they spur conversations.

Creating or entering a quote on Goodreads will have the same response. Take some time and pull some notable/memorable/thought-provoking quotes from your book. Make sure they are relatively short and not inside knowledge or, in other words, make sure they will be something that resonates with people who haven't read your book yet.

Submitting quotes from your book is a commonly overlooked function of Goodreads. It is a simple, yet powerful addition to your networking efforts.

To enter a quote on Goodreads, simply click on "Quotes" on the drop-down menu under Community, and then click on "Add A Quote" link in the upper right corner. Add the Quote, author, and most importantly, add some tags so it can be found by others. Enter as many tags as you find appropriate.

Ask the Author

The "Ask the Author" section is a relatively new addition to the Goodreads site and I've mentioned it previously. You can answer a pre-set selection of questions on your "Author Dashboard" and the answers will be visible to visitors. Goodreads also features a selection of authors and encourages readers to ask them a question. Make sure you fill out your questions and perhaps you will be chosen to be featured.

Trivia

Trivia questions are questions that people can try to answer in a multiple-choice format. The majority of these trivia questions are literary-related questions or questions based on very commonly read books. Although it is possible to add your own questions, I would suggest avoiding adding questions about your books, unless they are general enough that someone who has not read your book can guess at the answer. All answers are multiple-choice, so choosing the correct answer can be made relatively easy.

To add a question, look in the upper right for the "Add a Question" link. Fill out the information required, and when finished, click on the Submit Question button. The trivia questions will appear on the appropriate book/author page, so make sure you fill in the book/author information so it can appear where it belongs. Also, make sure your question appears in the Never-Ending Quiz. The default checkbox should be checked.

Take some time and play with the trivia questions. Some I found were quite challenging! See how much you remember from your high school Shakespeare class and see what types of questions other people add.

Quizzes

The next entry we get to on our list of Community functionality is Quizzes. Often Trivia and Quizzes are confused. They have the same guidelines, indicating they should both be about literary books, but Quizzes, in reality, are about all books and less about the classics.

Quizzes can be useful for connecting with readers. I feel that every author should plan to create a series of quiz questions for each of their books. Let's take a wander through this section.

Click on "Quizzes" on the list, and as you can see, there is quite a wide variety of quizzes available. Goodreads sorts the quizzes into various categories and they can also be searched by tag. Some of these quizzes are very popular and are taken by many readers. Looking at the Popular category, you can see that some of the quizzes have been taken hundreds of thousands of times. You may notice there are quizzes about authors, books, and general questions about genres—one of my favorites being about Greek mythology.

To create a quiz, click on the "Create a Quiz" link in the upper right. At first glance, you can see that a quiz has as many as ten questions and they are all multiple choice. The multiple-choice aspect makes it easy to guess at answers as well as determine the correctness of the answer. Every quiz needs a title and a description. Tags can be used so people that might be interested in it can find your quiz. If you are creating a quiz about one of your books, upload the cover graphic as an image and then start with your questions. You will notice that every question has a book/author link to allow you to connect your question properly. Any question/quiz that you associate with an author/book title (yours or another) will appear on the appropriate page for interested readers to answer or guess at the answer.

Once all the questions and answers have been entered, click on the "Create a Quiz" button to save your quiz. At this point, you can either wait for people to discover your quiz, or you can invite people to complete your quiz. We will talk about Events later in this chapter, but keep quizzes in mind when learning about Events. It is possible to invite your friends to take your quiz and even possible to award a prize to everyone who takes it as you can see who completes each quiz.

Use your creativity to find ways to engage your readers! Maybe you don't create a quiz about your book, but you create a quiz about research that you carried out when creating your book. Make it funny; make it engaging; encourage your readers to engage in your world!

Creative Writing

One thing many writers love about Goodreads is that creative writing can be posted on their profile. This is another great way of interacting with your fans. This section allows you to share samples of your writing as it is developing and get some feedback.

To enter a sample of your writing, click on "Creative Writing" on the drop-down menu under Community and then "My Writing" in the upper right corner and then "Get Started" on the next screen that appears. The fields that need to be filled in are straight-forward. Make sure that you enter appropriate tags so that your work can be found by people that have a potential interest in what you are sharing.

In a note on the right side of the entry page, Goodreads reminds you that you retain the rights to work that you share in this area, but you are giving Goodreads the right to make it available for reading according to their Terms of Use.

Take a few moments to look through the work that people have shared. It can be sorted by many different criteria as well as searched using tags. It is possible to look at the writing shared by your friends. If this is something that interests you, leave a sample of your writing, and comment on the writing of others.

People

The second last part of the Community section is "People." Click on this entry and see what there is to see. Goodreads is a place of networking and a place of readers sharing the books they read.

One of the questions I frequently get is concerning finding people to friend on Goodreads. I often have many answers to that question, but the People section can be a good choice. You can view people (account holders) sorted according to the following categories:

- Top readers
- Top reviewers
- Most popular reviewers
- Most followed
- Top librarians
- Recent reviews

The people who come up under each of these categories can be sorted into people from your country and the rest of the world with the idea that you might give preference to people from your own country. Some of these categories have the potential to be very useful in your networking activities. Others, not so much. Although it might be interesting to find out who the most popular reviewers or top reviewers are, they may not read the genre of your book. It can give you a starting point if you are looking for reviewers, however.

I recommend that you take some time and wander your way through the various groupings of people. You might find some potential friends or future reviewers of your book.

Events

Events are a popular feature. They can be used to inform your Goodreads friends of an online event, such as a blog tour or a price reduction for one of your books, as well as an in-person event like a book signing. We will do a quick review that covers all aspects of this feature but keep in mind that the event functionality is seen as an over-used part of Goodreads by many, with these little notifications often being viewed as spam.

Events are the last entry on the drop-down menu of Community items. An Event is similar in its use to a Facebook event. It allows for the entry of information and the invitation of friends to an event. I've created a screencast on the setup process of an event. Please view the video to help you with the steps.

Starting on the first page of the Events section, you will see that you can search for current events. Events, by default, are all public (unless that is changed) and searchable.

We are going to learn how to create an event, invite people, and then we will talk about searching for current events.

To add an event, look for the "Add an Event" link in the upper right corner and click on it. Take a quick peek through the fields of information that are needed and you'll see that this form has been created primarily for an in-person event. Since the majority of Events that are created are for online events, we will be ignoring some of the fields.

For this example, let's create an event for a 99 cent sale for your book. Start at the top and fill out the dates. The start date is the first date of your sale and the end date is the last date of your sale. If you fill out a date to RSVP and choose to send a reminder to people who respond, you will send non-responders 2 notifications which will potentially annoy them. I generally leave the RSVP date the same as the start date.

Give your event a catchy title that will encourage people to read the notification. Under Event Type, choose "Other." I suggest ignoring the physical location type of fields but entering your blog's URL for the details about your sale (and bring traffic to your blog). Create a description that is both detail-rich catchy enough to make people want to pick up a copy of your book. I'm not a fan of the RSVP system. You'll notice there are two check boxes. The first one allows the event to be public, and the second one allows other people to invite their friends. You want to leave both of these checked for our example. Note: it is possible to use Goodreads to send invites to a private event.

If an event is public, it can be searched for and found by anyone on Goodreads. Using our example of a book sale, you want as many people as possible to find out about it. That idea extends to the ability of others to invite their friends. Make it easy to spread the word about your sale.

The last step in creating the event is to click on the Save button at the bottom of the page. Once the event is saved, the next step is to invite people to your event. To do that, click on the Invite friends link and you will be supplied with a list of your friends, possibly in different categories. Go through the lists of friends, clicking on those you choose to invite. Goodreads has blocks in place to potentially stop you from spamming all your friends with an invite. There are ways around this.

I suggest inviting 200 friends at a time and logging out, and then back in between batches. Generally, Goodreads caps invites at 500/day, but inviting people in smaller amounts usually allows you to bypass that limit.

Once all your invites have been sent, you will have some people respond with a yes/no/maybe, and perhaps a comment, but the majority don't respond. Many people will, however, take action.

It is possible to see a list of events to which you have been invited (including your own) by clicking on "My Events" on the right-hand side of the screen. It is also possible to view "All Events." When you click on that link on the upper right-hand side of the screen, you will get a list of all public events. This is one good reason to create a public one. Anyone searching through the events can find yours.

Since the starting point for the Events page is the ability to search, play with this a bit and see if you can see what events are happening today, or in your country, etcetera. See what other people see. Perhaps find a giveaway to enter or a book that is on sale.

My final comment on Events is to reiterate what I said at the beginning. Many people view Events on Goodreads as spam. Use them sparingly. Certainly don't create an Event for every blog post! When they are used sparingly, they will have more of an impact than the events that are daily occurrences.

21

OTHER ASSORTED FUNCTIONALITY

Reading Challenges

Reading challenges can be great for several reasons:

- Other readers/friends can see what books you are reading
- Everyone that can see your books can add them to their lists.
- Because of the above two reasons, they are a great way to help authors publicize their books!

This is also another way for readers and fans to interact with their favorite authors.

To start a reading challenge, click on the "Home" link and look to the far right for your picture and click on it, looking for the "Reading Challenge" link and click on it. Starting a challenge is easy. Just choose how many books you want to read the next calendar year and click on "Start Challenge." You can grab a widget code to place on the sidebar of your blog to advertise the fact you are doing a Reading Challenge.

Reading Challenges are huge on Goodreads. Looking at the stats for the year 2021 as I'm writing this book, I see that 2,439,326 people are participating this year, and so far 22,974,021 books have been read. What a great networking potential!

Challenges have the following additional important points:

- People can leave comments for you and ask about other books
- You can change your book goal if you change your mind through the year
- You can view your own list to track your progress

Consider starting a Reading Challenge this year and every year. Not only keep track of the books you are reading but help other authors out at the same time. Authors who join in the challenge are not only helping themselves but other authors as well. You will be promoting the books you are reading. When other members see your list, they will be more likely to add these books to their own shelves. Remember, you want your books to be added to the 'To-read" shelf to help its rankings.

Goodreads Advertising

There are mixed feelings about Goodreads Advertising. When the first edition of the book was written in 2013, I participated in what they then called "Self-Serve Advertising." This allowed me to spend a small amount of money to make my books a bit more visible. This type of advertising has since been ended and the only type of advertising that remains is high-end, hands-on help with launch activities and other such advertising. There are no prices on the website and I would assume that the price is certainly out of my budget. If this is something that you are interested in exploring, there is a contact form that can be filled out here: https://www.goodreads.-com/advertisers and someone will get in touch with you to discuss.

22

WIDGETS

Because I feel Widgets are a very important part of the Goodreads networking functionality, I want to go over all the widgets available one more time.

There are Reader widgets and Author widgets. To find the reader widgets, click on your picture in the upper right to show the drop-down menu and click on "Account Settings" and then click on "Edit my User Profile." Once that page opens, you will see a label of Widgets. These widgets are specialized for readers to display what they are reading and their attachment to Goodreads. The available widgets are email widgets (which will share the book you are currently reading as part of an email signature), a bookshelf widget, an updates widget, a grid widget, a quote widget, a reading challenge widget, and a group widget. The email widget will share your latest read with people that you email. The bookshelf and grid widget will display a specific selection of books. The "Update" widget will display your latest activity. I feel this is only appropriate for readers that are very active on Goodreads. A quote widget is a cool way to display a quote from one of your books, and lastly, a Group widget is a great idea for a very active group.

Let's look at the "Author" widget selection. To find them, click on your picture in the upper right and click on the "Author Dashboard." From that page, look down the right side for Author Widgets and click on it. Looking at the page of available author widgets, you will see Goodreads buttons of various sizes, Review widgets, Add to My Books widget, and Books widget. The use of the buttons is obvious; they are essentially what I would call a follow icon. If you put that on your blog and someone clicks on it, they are brought directly to your author profile and can friend or follow. The "Review" widget will display a couple of snippets from reviews left for a specific book. The "Add to My Books" widget is something you would combine with a book display to encourage people to add that book to a shelf on their Goodreads account. I don't really like this widget as I find many authors have difficulty getting it to display well. The "Books" widget allows an author to display their books along with some details about the book. I find this encourages readers to investigate books they find interesting.

The last type of widget, a "Giveaway" Widget, is only appropriate if you have a giveaway on the go. It can be found on the giveaway page as well.

Where I hear a lot of complaints is around the configuration and set up of the widgets. For some reason, not all widgets are manipulated in the same way. I believe they can all be figured out. Except for the Follow button, all of the widgets require the input of some information or some choices to be made. Once this part has been completed, there is some code offered that can be copied and pasted into a text widget/gadget on the sidebar of your blog, or directly into a post or page. The video on widgets in the course associated with this book will help you not only configure a widget but also learn how to put it in place on either a WordPress or Blogger blog.

So why do I like the widgets so much? The simple answer is that it is an easy way to invite participation by the readers of your blog. Whether you choose to advertise some reviews you are proud of, some books of your fellow authors on a particular shelf, or simply a display of the books you have published, Goodreads makes it easy to do. I encourage you to look at the selection of widgets and think about how you can use them to your advantage.

CONCLUSION

I'd like to thank you for letting me share my love of Goodreads with you. I hope the combination of book and video course has helped you better understand not only how to navigate the site, but how to take advantage of all the various functionalities Goodreads offers authors. If you haven't had a chance to view the videos I have available for you, the link again is http://the-author-s-technical-help-desk.teachable.com/p/author-guide-to-goodreads. Access to this is free. Enjoy!

In today's world of book sales, all authors need book reviews from readers posted to the various online retailers. Since you picked up one of my books, I am assuming you are an author - a writer. I encourage you to post an honest review of this book, when you are finished, to the retail site you purchased it from. This action you will help you experience what you will ask your readers to do. It is easier to ask this of your readers if you understand the process.

Thank you so much!

ACKNOWLEDGMENTS

As I said in the dedication, this book took a community to get it published.

Many thanks to my mom, Gwynnith Smith for continuously copy editing all the editions of this book. Every time I headed in a somewhat new direction, she took her virtual red pen to my work.

YOUR HELPFUL HINTS ARE WAITING...

Interested in getting some helpful hints and some helpful videos to your inbox? As I'm sure you are aware, authors are encouraged to give away a free book to encourage people to join their mailing lists.

My books are different - they solve a problem. Just because you picked up one of my books doesn't mean you want a free book on a completely different topic. Because of this, I offer subscribers to my mailing list, free help - usually in the form of blog posts or YouTube Videos. I let everyone know about new releases and offer money off of my online courses.

If this sounds like something you would be interested in, join me at: http://bakerviewconsulting.com/reader-list/

ABOUT THE AUTHOR

Social Media and Wordpress Consultant Barb Drozdowich has taught in colleges, universities and in the banking industry. More recently, she brings her many years of teaching experience and a deep love of books to help authors develop the social media platform needed to succeed in today's fast evolving publishing world. She delights in taking technical subjects and making them understandable by the average person. She owns Bakerview Consulting and manages the popular blog, Sugarbeat's Books, where she talks about Romance novels.

She is the author of 27 books, over 60 YouTube videos, and 6 online courses all focused on helping authors and bloggers. Barb lives in the mountains of British Columbia with her family.

Barb can be found on her Book Blog, Business Blog, Pinterest, Goodreads, and Youtube

As well as:

barbdrozdowich.com
barb@bakerviewconsulting.com

ALSO BY BARB DROZDOWICH

All my books start with a problem that needs a solution - with a group of authors letting me know about a subject that they don't understand. I take it, break it down and see if I can add some clarity.

The books I've written attack the subjects of:

1) Understanding the world of Book Bloggers, Book Reviewers and book reviews

2) Understanding all the parts and pieces of an author's online presence at a beginner's level

3) Understand the world of book promotions

4) Understanding What to blog, How to blog and Why to blog for authors

5) Understand how to use Goodreads as a tool of networking and communication with readers

6) Understand mailing lists and newsletters

7) Understand how to self-publish a book regardless of what country you live in

8) Understand how to improve your website

During a recent workshop I gave on self-publishing, I walked participants through an exercise to help them understand the power of e-readers as well as the limits of e-readers. I was talking about the fact that not all e-readers can make use of clickable links as not all are connected to the internet or have browser capabilities. We also talked about creating links that readers from a variety of countries can actually use - my example was around solely using an Amazon.com link. Suddenly the light went in my own head about all of the clickable links I put in my books. So…going forward I'm directing everyone to a page that contains information about all of my books and buy links that are associated with those books. The link is easy to type in manually or click on if you have the ability. It is: https://readerlinks.com/mybooks/733

All of my books are also found on my business blog (http://bakerviewconsulting.com) and my author website (http://barbdrozdowich.com).

4 of my books are permanently free.

My books are:

The Author's Guide to Working with Book Bloggers

The Author's On-Line Presence

The Author's Guide to Book Promotion

The Book Blogger Platform

The Author's Guide to Goodreads

Blogging for Authors

The Complete Mailing List Toolkit

Strategies to Grow Your List

Newsletters That Rock

Get Your Emails Delivered

The Author's Guide to Self-Publishing for Canadians

How to Self-Publish a Book

Book Reviews for Author Success

Website Tips & Tricks

How to Optimize Your Social Media

How to Target Book Blogger for Optimize Results

Top Advice for Authors Promoting Their Books

Book Blogger Survey

On-Line Video Courses:

As thanks for reading one of my books, I offer a coupon for 50% off any of my courses. The website that describes all my courses is Author's Tech School

(http://authorstechschool.com) Use code ICANLEARN at checkout.

WordPress for Beginners

Are you an author or blogger who struggles with the technical side of your website? Do you wish you could change the layout of your website but are afraid you'll break it?

In "WordPress for Beginners," you'll learn how to build a beautiful, functional website in WordPress. This course is designed just for authors or bloggers who have little to no technical experience, so you don't need any prior knowledge. Your instructor, Barb Drozdowich, uses easy-to-follow directions with specific examples so you'll be able to get started on your website right away.

When you sign up for "WordPress for Beginners," you'll get immediate access to more than 8 hours of content covering topics such as:

- Choosing a hosting company and get your website going
- Understanding the basics of WordPress: logging in, layouts, settings, etc.
- Using themes and plugins
- Protecting your site from hackers and spammers
- Making sure your website looks great on any browser or phone
- Backing up your website

Once you have the basics down, there are even a few advanced topics to build upon what you've learned, like using Google Analytics to track your content performance and setting up search engine optimization (SEO).

If you are an author or blogger looking to build a brand-new website or enhance the one you already have, don't let your lack of confidence stop you. Sign up and get started on that shiny new site today! The shortened link to the course is: https://geni.us/kY7K4L

WordPress Dot Com for Beginners

Whether you're looking to start a blog or put together a website for your small business, figuring out how to actually get going can feel like a tall task.

But it doesn't have to be.

In "WordPress.com for Beginners," you'll learn everything you need to know to get a website up and running on the free version of WordPress. The course includes 25 easy-to-understand videos that guide you through each step, from creating an account to setting up your site to publishing your first post.

When you sign up for "WordPress.com for Beginners," you'll get immediate access to more than 3 hours of content covering topics such as:

- Setting up your WordPress.com account
- The difference between pages and posts and how to publish content on them
- A walk-through of 4 different themes and how to use them on your website
- How to manage comments and give other people access to your website
- What are widgets and how can they improve your site

There are even a few freebies and plenty of other resources along the way to set you up for success.

If you've made the decision to launch your own website, don't let the technology scare you away. Sign up today and start publishing your content in no time! The shortened link to the course is: https://geni.us/P9zt8

Mailerlite for Beginners

If you sell a product or offer a service, you should also have a mailing list. It's the best way to get information out to your audience, share offers, and turn enthusiastic fans into paying customers. People who have signed up for your newsletter are already interested in what you have to say and are much more likely to pay attention to what you have to offer than if they stumble across an ad on social media.

Once you start collecting email addresses, you'll want to sign up for a newsletter service that can send customized emails to multiple people at a time.

In "Mailerlite for Beginners," you'll learn all about one of the simpler newsletter services, Mailerlite. Your instructor, Barb Drozdowich, will walk you through the steps from how to navigate the dashboard, how to create a campaign (a newsletter), how to create signup forms, and more.

When you sign up, you'll have immediate access to 19 videos that cover everything you need to know to get started, such as:

- The legalities you need to know about (opt-ins and opt-outs, what the GDPR is and what it means for you)
- How to set up your account
- Managing your subscribers
- How to create a campaign and send out a newsletter
- How to run reports to see what percentage of people are opening your emails and clicking on the links within your newsletters

You'll also get plenty of resources for more information and support once the course is over.

Learning something new can feel overwhelming, but it doesn't have to be. Sign up and start connecting with your potential customers today! The shortened link to the course is: https://geni.us/MLbeginner

---

How to Self-Publish a Book

Each year, more and more authors are realizing that they don't have to take the traditional publishing route to get their work out into the world. Self-publishing is a great option for many writers, but the actual process of publishing a book yourself can feel overwhelming.

So overwhelming that you might not ever get started in the first place.

In "How to Self-Publish a Book," you'll learn everything from putting together your manuscript to getting an ISBN number to formatting and distributing your book. The easy-to-understand, step-by-step format will guide you through the entire process. Before you know it, you'll be sharing your brand new book with your friends and family!

When you sign up for "How to Self-Publish a Book", you'll get immediate access to 19 videos (more than two hours of content!) that cover key topics such as:

• How the publishing industry has changed and what that means for potential authors

• All aspects of publishing: Writing, editing, designing, formatting, uploading, marketing

• What you need to know about file formats

• The necessary pieces to include in a book file

• Where to sell your book

• Red flags to look for if you go with a self-publishing service

Plus, plenty of additional links and resources along the way for even more information.

Don't let what you don't know stop you. Sign up today and finally become the published author you've always dreamed of! The shortened link to the course is: https://geni.us/SelfPublish

Website Tips & Tricks - 15 Lessons to Supercharge Your Author Website

You've finally figured out how to create a website to promote your book—great! But once you set it up, how will people find you? What are readers looking for anyway? How do you fix it if something looks off?

The answers are easier than you think.

In "Website Tips & Tricks," you'll gain access to a ton of useful skills to build upon the foundation you already have and maintain your site throughout the years. It's designed for authors who have very little technical knowledge, and you can implement what you learn right away.

Just a few of the topics include:

• The three pages your website absolutely must have

- Choosing your theme and plugins
- Creating content that is reader-friendly and highlights your books
- Setting up your website so it loads faster
- Improving your website's visibility in searches

Most importantly, you'll become comfortable playing around with your website.

Your instructor is Barb Drozdowich, who has published 27 books on a variety of tech topics, including 7 about software and technology. She teaches several online courses and has 50+ YouTube videos, all focusing on making technology easier for beginners to understand. She breaks complex topics down into simple steps so that you can use what you learn right away.

Managing your website doesn't have to be scary. Sign up for immediate access to "Website Tips & Tricks" and start improving your site today! The shortlink to the course is: https://geni.us/WebsiteSupercharge

A SNEAK PEAK AT BLOGGING FOR AUTHORS

What is Blogging?

AT ITS HEART, blogging is just another form of communication. In my mind there isn't a lot of difference between blogging and having a chat with some friends over a cup of coffee. You'll notice that I'm using the words "chat" or "conversation." When we're talking about blogging, I want you to keep the word "dialogue" in mind.

A blog is neither a billboard, nor a monologue. Blogging should be a dialogue.

Although I refer to the words "conversation" and "dialogue," your first response may be that no one talks on your blog, or that no one leaves comments for you to respond to. Times have changed.

The face of a conversation has changed in the electronic world. The person with whom we are chatting may not literally respond with words – they might respond with actions such as sharing your post with their friends on Facebook. They are doing the electronic equivalent of "Come over here and listen to this person." The electronic version is more along the lines of "This is great information; please go and read it." That's a response and in the big picture, that's a much more important response. Although I'm the first one to admit that comments are wonderful, such interaction is between two people. I have 16,000+ followers on Twitter. If I share on Twitter, it's pretty likely that more people than just myself will be part of the conversation. It's also pretty likely that a handful of my 16,000+ followers will join in, in their own way.

If you have a WordPress blog, one of the people you are "speaking" to might click on the Like button or in fact be so moved by what you have to say that they re-blog it. And the conversation grows to include even more people.

The author's blog is a space that belongs to the author – unlike Facebook, Twitter or other social media. The author's blog is also searched and indexed by Google unlike the various social media (for the most part). This allows for your conversations to be searched for and found long after they take place. This isn't true of any material that you put on most social media. In fact, a post on your blog can be found years after it's created. The accepted shelf life of a Facebook post is considered to be between two and five hours and the shelf life of a Twitter post is 18 minutes. A LinkedIn post can have a shelf life of up to 24 hours in some cases.

An author's blog is the place where the author can share with their community; the place they can start or continue conversations and have dialogues. This is the place that the dialogue will grow a community of friends and supporters – people with like interests who will help spread the word about your book.

The content shared is based on the author's personality and interests and should be reflective of their branding. Yup – there's that nasty word – branding. We'll talk about branding – how straightforward it is – and how it's often blown out of proportion. We'll flesh out the topic of what to blog about, but first of all, we'll talk about why.

Why Do I Need to Blog?

THE QUESTION that comes up repeatedly during my discussions with authors – Why? Why do I need to blog? There are several answers to this question. At the top of the heap, blogging is a writing exercise, another opportunity to develop that writing muscle. The second reason is to communicate with your readers and develop a community.

We all figured out how to make friends in Kindergarten: "Hi, my name is Barb. Do you want to play with me?" As adults in the electronic world, the way to make friends is admittedly a bit more complicated, but not impossible. It goes something along the lines of, "Hi, my name is Barb and I write books. Let's explore interests we have in common and chat about stuff over a cup of virtual coffee."

The third reason, as I mentioned in the previous section, is to communicate and share with your community of readers in a fairly permanent way. Unlike the other parts of your platform, your blog posts can be searched and found months or years after they were first shared. So a post that attracted a new reader into having a virtual chat with you two years ago could easily be found today and have the same effect on a new reader.

Your blog is your public face to the world. In today's society if we want to find out more about a public figure, we "Google" them. Frankly, we expect all public figures including authors to have a website of some sort where we can find out more about them and their books. As we'll find out in the coming chapters, it's important to have a blog, but generally not necessary to have a website *and* a blog. A blog offers an author the ability to add fresh content on a regular basis to their site – something that Google LOVES!

Think of Google as a toddler. For those parents reading this, you realize that toddlers don't stay interested in anything for long. Even shiny, new toys are quickly abandoned for the box they came in. Google is similar. Google is attracted to new content. A blog that's posted to on a regular basis provides a steady stream of "shiny new toys" for the Google search engine. This helps a site rise up the ranks in a Google search. While it's true that the majority of your traffic will initially either come from your friends or be referral traffic from other social media, you want readers to be able to Google the genre they read and find your site in a search. We'll talk more about this in a future chapter.

One last comment for this section is about tone and language. As

I've mentioned previously, I feel that your blog should be a conversation – a dialogue with your readers. A blog post that's a dialogue with your readers is typically casual in its language and tone, like a conversation between friends. It's meant to share information as you would over a cup of coffee or a glass of beer with your friends. If your blog post is more formal, it will sound like a dissertation or even a monologue. It may end up conveying information to an audience, but it typically won't turn your audience into a community. In short, your audience will react differently. Think about how you react when reading let's say a Wikipedia page. You're looking for information and you get it. Compare this to reading a chatty, personalized blog post. You'll have a different internal reaction.

I'll continue to remind you to keep the word "dialogue" in your mind as we go through this book. I find when you think of something as a dialogue, that is what you create.

To continue reading, pick up a copy of Blogging for Authors from various retailers: https://readerlinks.com/mybooks/733

Made in the USA
Monee, IL
04 November 2026

67381917R00069